Church Growth

...it is possible!

DAG HEWARD-MILLS

Parchment House

First published 2011 by Parchment House
3rd Printing 2014

Find out more about Dag Heward-Mills at:

Healing Jesus Campaign
Write to: evangelist@daghewardmills.org
Healing Jesus Campaign
Website: www.daghewardmills.org
Facebook: Dag Heward-Mills
Twitter: @EvangelistDag

ISBN: 978-9988-8500-6-7

Contents

Foreword

I would like to highly recommend the new book on "Church Growth" written by our dear friend and "Church Growth International" Board Member Dr. Dag Heward-Mills.

I have known Dr. Heward-Mills now for many years, and he has been a faithful participant and honored member of our Board, and we are so glad to endorse his book on "Church Growth". He has studied and researched this subject for many years, and he has evidence of his great success on this subject.

Dr. Heward-Mills writes many articles for our "Church Growth" Magazine which reveals his literary talents, his deep knowledge of the Word of God, and his many applications of church growth. His tremendous ministry demonstrates every aspect of practical church growth throughout the world.

Dr. Heward-Mills has a rare talent in being able to articulate the many areas of expertise that he has gained in his own life and his "Lighthouse Chapel International" Ministries in countless cities around the world. He is the Founder and Bishop of these "Lighthouse Chapels" which are growing up in every location around the globe.

His new book on "Church Growth" will give you a thorough, practical and inspirational understanding of how the local church can become an international Ministry for thousands of people who are seeking the Lord Jesus Christ. Dr. Heward-Mills' new book will provide you with a step-by-step manual on how to make the growth of your church an exciting adventure based on the multifaceted works of Jesus Christ in His Body, The Church.

December 10, 2010

Dr. David Yonggi Cho
Chairman
Church Growth International
Seoul, South Korea

Section 1

CHURCH GROWTH AND
A BURNING DESIRE

Chapter 1

Church Growth and
a Burning Desire

Where there is no vision ...

Proverbs 29:18

Does a Vision Really Lead
to Church Growth?

Many years ago, I read from David Yonggi Cho's magazine about how it was important to have a vision and a dream for church growth. I never understood why and how a vision was necessary for church growth.

Dr David Yongi Cho, the pastor of the largest church in the world and propagator of the concept of church growth, said something else that I did not understand. He said, "Your vision makes you. You do not make your vision." I also did not understand this.

Honestly, I assumed that the subject "having a vision" was always mentioned as a standard opening point for all teachings on leadership.

As I listened to people teaching about the importance of having a vision, writing down goals, etc., I still did not understand how it brought about church growth. Every pastor who attended church growth conferences seemed full of visions and desires for church growth.

I thought to myself, "But all pastors have a desire for their churches to grow, but their churches still do not grow. If it were desires and visions that led to church growth, then every church would be a big church!"

Your Vision Must Be
a Burning Vision

As the years have gone by, I have realized that the vision you have must be a burning vision. You cannot have a superficial vision for a large church. A shallow vision will not make your church grow. The vision must eat you up and burn within your soul. Then, all the things Dr Cho said will happen. That burning vision will literally make you into a mega church pastor.

Actually, in the absence of a burning vision for a large church you will never have real church growth.

The way a burning vision causes church growth is by inspiring and leading you on the difficult road to real church growth in a way that no human being can.

A Burning Vision Becomes the Invisible Engine
of All Church Growth

It is a long and tortuous journey to become the pastor of a large church.

A burning vision and dream is the invisible engine that drives a minister on that journey from being the pastor of a small church to becoming the pastor of a mega church.

Some pastors do not have that internal engine that is needed to make them do the many hard and difficult things necessary for church growth.

External Influence Cannot Make You
a Mega Church Pastor

There is no external advice or input that can sufficiently drive an individual on that difficult road to becoming a mega church pastor. All external influences will fade out long before you become a mega church pastor. External advice, encouragement and counsel are too short-lived to cause any minister of the gospel to survive on the road to church growth.

What a Vision Can Make You Do

There is something that a burning internal vision and dream does for you that no human being can do for you.

The internal burning vision and dream makes you humble enough to do all the things that you must to have church growth.

A burning vision and dream for a large church makes you pray for church growth. Without a burning vision and dream you will never pray hard enough to attract God's attention.

A burning vision and dream for a large church makes you seek the wisdom and strategies needed for church growth. Without a burning vision and dream, you will not spend the time needed to seek the wisdom that brings church growth. You will soon be irritated with the strategies that are taught by church growth pastors. Without a burning vision you will say that these teachings do not work.

The internal burning vision and dream will cause you to keep reading and re-reading the same things until something works.

Without a burning vision and dream for a large church, you will have no time to read the books that lead to church growth.

A burning vision and dream for a large church will drive you to meet the people who will help you to have church growth. It will make you humble enough to relate with and fellowship with the right people until their influence and anointing rubs off on you.

Without a burning vision and dream for a large church you will not listen to the messages that bring church growth. You will criticize the very thing that you need most and even make fun of it.

A burning vision and dream is the only true source of the staying power, stamina and persistence needed for the long journey towards church growth.

Section 2

CHURCH GROWTH AND LAY PEOPLE

Chapter 2

How You Can Achieve Great Things through Lay People

Laikos – The Layman

History teaches us that great things can be accomplished through people who "lack skills". A quick glance at the achievements of lay people or common people will inspire you to use them to make your church grow.

The word layman comes from the Greek word laikos which means "having no skills". The following are a few definitions of the word layman.

1. A layman is an ordinary person.
2. A layman is a normal person.
3. A layman is a commonplace person.
4. A layman is a usual person.
5. A layman is a regular person.
6. A layman is a common person.
7. A layman is an everyday person.
8. A layman is an average person.
9. A layman is someone who is not a professional.
10. A layman is someone who is not an expert.
11. A layman is someone who is not specialized.
12. A layman is someone who is not skilled.
13. A layman is someone who is not trained.
14. A layman is someone who is not certified.
15. A layman is someone who is not licensed.

Great Achievements in the Church World

1. Lay people were the pillars of the great reformation of the church.

Martin Luther's translation of the Bible into the language of the common people changed the world. Instead of just being in Latin, the Bible was made more accessible to the common people.

Once the common/lay people had revelation knowledge in their hands they changed the world. Realising that salvation was available to all men through the grace of God they rose up and championed what we now know as the Reformation.

2. Lay people are the pillars of the great Methodist Church.

By the middle of the 20th century, Methodism was the largest Protestant denomination in the United States. The great Methodist church has ridden on the backs of lay people.

A very early tradition of preaching in the Methodist churches was for a Lay Preacher to be appointed to lead services of worship and preach in a group of churches called a "circuit".

The lay preacher walked or rode on horseback in a prescribed circuit of the preaching places according to an agreed pattern and timing.

After the appointment of ministers and pastors, this lay preaching tradition continued with ''Methodist Local Preachers'' being appointed by individual churches, and in turn approved and invited by nearby churches, as an adjunct to the minister or during their planned absences.

3. Lay people were the pillars of the largest single church in the world.

One of the foundational principles on which the Yoido Full Gospel Church is built is the principle of working through lay people.

The Yoido Full Gospel Church, founded by David Yonggi Cho and his mother-in-law, Choi Ja-shil, both Assemblies of God pastors held its maiden worship service on May 15, 1958 with four other ladies in the home of Choi Ja-shil.

Membership of the church had reached fifty thousand by 1977, a figure that doubled in only two years. On 30 November 1981, membership topped two hundred thousand. By this time, it was the largest single congregation in the world and was recognized as such by the Los Angeles Times.

In 2007 its membership stood at 830,000, with seven Sunday services translated into sixteen languages.

4. Lay people are the pillars of huge networks of churches originating from Nigeria and Ghana.

Both The Redeemed Christian Church of God with its home in Nigeria and The Church of Pentecost with its headquarters in Ghana are known to make good use of lay people. Both of these ministries have huge networks of churches and regularly employ the services of lay people for preaching and pastoring.

The Church of Pentecost was founded by an Irish missionary sent by the Apostolic Church, Bradford, UK to the then Gold Coast.

It has grown to have a membership of over 1.7 million members; the Church of Pentecost has over 13,000 churches in 70 countries across all the continents of the world.

In 1952, the Redeemed Christian Church of God was founded in Nigeria by Pa Josiah Akindayomi.

Under the leadership of its General Overseer, Reverend E.A. Adeboye, it has grown to have churches in more than 140 countries, with millions in attendance.

Truly, these are great achievements and they have been made possible through the inputs of lay people.

Great Achievements in the Secular World

1. The great government system of democracy was birthed through lay people.

Democracy is giving common people the opportunity to act and change the government if they wish.

Democracy is the common man's power to refuse to live under unacceptable conditions.

Democracy is the common man's participation and influence in a country.

Democracy is built upon the principle of equal opportunity given to all common people.

2. The great super-power was given birth to through lay people.

The American Revolution is a classic example of the power of the common or lay people in shaping history.

The common man gave birth to a superpower. At the turn of the last century, the American Revolution was a successful experiment that marked the transition of a world controlled by a few to a world controlled by the many.

The Revolution was largely shaped by small revolutionary organizations such as the Sons of Liberty. These organizations were not controlled by the rich and powerful landowners but common people of average social status came together to plant the seeds of the Revolution.

3. The great election victory came through lay people.

In May 2008, Barack Obama first black president of the United States of America, clenched the Democratic nomination for the presidency of the United States.

Even though the country's rich and influential Democrats were Clinton supporters and provided the millions of dollars, Obama raised more than any other presidential candidate in history by using the power of the common person.

Obama raised over $80 million in his campaign, most of which came from common people making small individual contributions.

Chapter 3

How Lay People Have Helped Churches to Grow

I have experienced two worlds of ministry — full-time ministry and lay ministry. Most pastors are only aware of the existence of the full-time dimension of ministry. My intention is to help you to discover the reality of how lay people can cause the church to grow.

A lay person is someone who maintains his secular job and yet is active in the ministry of the Lord Jesus. A full-time minister is someone who has abandoned his secular job to concentrate fully on the ministry.

Many ministers who are in full-time ministry are not comfortable with the idea of lay people participating in the ministry. This is because they want to maintain the ministry as the exclusive preserve of a few "called" men of God.

Some full-time ministers do not want to accept the reality that lay people are capable of making a substantial (non-financial) contribution to ministry. Many full-time ministers are happy to maintain their lay people as mere financial supporters.

Pastors want to feel special as they perform their exclusive ministerial duties. "Why should a lay person do what I do?" they say. They think, "After all, if you can do the job I'm doing, what makes me special? What makes me (the pastor) different if lay people can do the things I do?"

Many ministers are not convinced that lay people can do the work of the ministry. I have had pastors ask me, "Will they have time to attend to the needs of the flock?", and "Can they handle emergencies?" "Can they minister powerfully the way we do?"

The answer to these is very simple - a resounding YES! I have been in the lay ministry for many years and have found it to be practically possible.

I'm writing this book to introduce you to an alternative to the traditional concept of full-time priests who only wait on God in the temple. The lay ministry is a key to church growth. Churches that have experienced phenomenal growth have all employed the principle of using lay people for the ministry. I believe that it is the key to fulfilling the Great Commission. There is no way we are going to win this world with a few priests and pastors. Everyone must get involved. Many people must get involved at a higher ministerial level. There must be a revival of the lay ministry in the church.

There is such a thing as a lay pastor, i.e., a pastor who combines both his secular job and does the ministry as well. Ninety percent of the pastors in my church are lay pastors.

Full-time pastors must be secure in their positions in order to encourage lay people to get involved. There is nothing mystical about the ministry! There are pastors who want the ministry to be shrouded in mystery so that their members feel dependent on them.

It is time to demystify the art of shepherding and pastoring people. It is something that many can get involved with. What a blessing it is for lay people to discover that they can be useful in the ministry! What a blessing for the pastor when he discovers that the contributions of lay people can make his church grow.

I am not saying that there is no need for full-time ministers. I am myself a full-time minister. There is a great need for full-time ministers to be one hundred percent involved in ministry work. There are things that only full-time ministers can do.

I Was a Lay Pastor

At the age of about fifteen, in secondary school, I met the Lord. From the day I gave my life to Christ, I became very active in ministry. I was involved in soul winning and following up converts. I was also involved in singing and playing musical instruments for the Lord.

In the first phase of my Christian life, I was not a traditional Sunday morning church attendee. In fact, I hardly went to church on Sundays. My Christian life was so active from Monday to Saturday that I ended up resting on Sundays! On Mondays and Wednesdays I had a prayer meeting and Bible study. On Tuesdays and Thursdays I had music rehearsals. On Fridays we had fasting and prayer meetings. And then on Saturdays we would have a retreat from ten in the morning until six in the evening.

Whilst I was involved in these activities I never gave up my schooling. I completed my GCE 'O' levels and passed with a distinction - I had seven ones (one is the highest mark of distinction). That was a great accomplishment by any standards. In my GCE 'A' levels I topped my class and was one of the only people from my school admitted into the medical school. Throughout this period, I was fully involved in ministry. I preached! I won souls! I visited people in their homes! I counselled many people! I fasted and prayed! At one point, I fasted so much that I became as thin as a rake. Someone even asked me, "Do you think that you will get to Heaven by being a skeleton?"

Never did it occur to me that I had to be paid for the ministry work that I was involved in. By the time I was nineteen years old, I was fully involved in the ministry. I had many sheep who looked up to me for direction and prayer. By 1980 I was a strong preacher and leader of the Scripture Union fellowship. The point I am making is that ministry is possible alongside other pursuits.

I entered the university in October 1982. I was privileged to be studying medicine - one of the most difficult and time-consuming courses. Whilst in the university I began a Christian fellowship that is still in existence today.

During my fourth year, I began to establish the foundations for a church. I then became a pastor and was acknowledged as such whilst I was still a medical student.

During this time I was not being paid by anyone to do the work of the ministry. Neither did I slacken in my academic work. On the contrary, I did extremely well and won prizes in the medical school. I applied wisdom and sacrificed my leisure time so that I could be involved in ministry.

Sacrifice and Wisdom

These are the two keys to being in the lay ministry - *sacrifice and wisdom.*

What is the main task of a pastor? Is it to perform funerals and to officiate weddings? Certainly not! These are certainly duties of a minister but they are not main duties. If your ministry has deteriorated to the point where your main functions are to conduct marriages and bury people, then you need to read your Bible again! The main duty of a minister is to fulfil the Great Commission.

Go ye therefore, and teach all nations, baptizing them in the name of the Father, and of the Son, and of the Holy Ghost: Teaching them to observe all things whatsoever I have commanded you: and, lo, I am with you alway, even unto the end of the world. Amen.

Matthew 28:19, 20

The reason why it is called the Great Commission is because it is the great commandment to all ministers. It is sad to see ministers of the Gospel who have become mere social functionaries. Sometimes pastors are under pressure to be accepted by society.

As a result, they want to do nice things that relate to health, education, etc., so that they may gain the approval of society.

Apostle Peter came under the same pressure to leave his principal duties and to perform mainly social tasks.

And in those days, when the number of the disciples was multiplied, there arose a murmuring of the Grecians against the Hebrews, because their widows were neglected in the daily ministration. Then the twelve called the multitude of the disciples unto them, and said, It is not reason that we should leave the word of God, and serve tables.

Wherefore, brethren, look ye out among you seven men of honest report, full of the Holy Ghost and wisdom, whom we may appoint over this business. BUT WE WILL GIVE OURSELVES CONTINUALLY TO PRAYER, AND TO THE MINISTRY OF THE WORD.

Acts 6:1-4

You can see from this Scripture that Peter's main duty was to pray and to minister the Word. This is something that can be done by lay people.

Lay people can be taught to visit and counsel younger Christians!

Lay people can be taught how to preach!

Lay people can be taught how to witness!

Lay people can be taught how to minister the Word with power!

Lay people can be taught to make spiritual gains through prayer!

What I have just described is the work of a pastor. Any honest reader will agree that a lay person can become a lay pastor. What you need is a systematic way of training your lay people to become ministers. Do not limit your lay people because they are professionals in other fields. Do not say that your doctors, lawyers, architects, carpenters, engineers, tailors, masons, nurses and secretaries, cannot be pastors. They can!!

I remember visiting one of our churches that was pastored by a female nurse. There were hundreds of people in the church and I gave glory to God for that.

In a large house there are many vessels. God is using all kinds of people. Do not limit God to what you have been used to.

But in a great house there are not only vessels of gold and of silver, but also of wood and of earth; and some to honour, and some to dishonour. If a man therefore purge himself from these, he shall be a vessel unto honour, sanctified, and meet for the master's use, and prepared unto every good work.

2 Timothy 2:20, 21

When I was in my first year at the university, I was told by the Christian fellowship that *I could not be a leader because I was a medical student.* Medical students were considered too busy to be involved in ministry work. How unfortunate! They had effectively eliminated a whole group of potential leaders from the fellowship.

This is what many pastors do. They look at the doctors in the church and think to themselves, "Sit down quietly, receive your Sunday sermons and pay your tithes. Be a nice principled Christian doctor who does not perform abortions and you will please God!!"

I want you to know that a doctor can also please God by winning souls. It is true that God wants principled doctors. But God also wants doctors who will win souls and do the work of ministry. Today, I have doctors who own clinics and at the same time pastor churches with hundreds of members.

There are many architects who do full-time architectural work and are very fruitful in ministry. There are pastors who work in banks but pastor large churches. I have seen teachers, pharmacists, university lecturers, accountants, students, doctors, nurses, army officers, civil servants, air conditioner repairers, computer scientists, computer technicians, businessmen, and lawyers become great lay pastors.

Many people cannot believe that our long lists of pastors are lay people who are not paid by the church. If pastors understand that their lay people can do much more than just give money to the church, they would help themselves and their churches a great deal. That is what this section is about - showing how lay people can help the church to grow.

Please do not misunderstand me; not every layperson must become a pastor. Some of the lay people can function as ordinary shepherds (cell leaders). But there are others who have the call of God upon their lives and who will become pastors.

The Pineapple Patch

One day as I was walking on a hillside I saw something that I want to share with you. I was praying in tongues and walking along a footpath on one of the hills in Ghana. The entire hillside was covered with wild bushes and tall untamed grass. As I walked along, I saw a section within the wild grass measuring about 20 meters by 20 meters. In that particular section there were neatly planted pineapple plants. I could see the baby pineapples sprouting. That section of the hillside was very different from everywhere else.

The Spirit of the Lord spoke to me and said, "That section of the hillside is different because certain seeds have been planted there. That area of the hillside is different because some special investment has been made on that patch of ground."

The Lord told me that the rest of the hillside can be likened to the general congregation which receives seeds of normal preaching. The special patch of ground that was yielding pineapples could be likened to the part of the church that received the special seeds of leadership and pastoral training.

If you sow the seeds of pastoral training you will soon have many more pastors and leaders around you.

Many people do not invest the seeds that give rise to leaders, pastors and shepherds. If you sow the seeds that train leaders, you will harvest a crop of well-seasoned leaders. I spend more time with my leaders than I do with the general congregation.

The teachings in this book are examples of some of the things I have taught ordinary people over the years.

This investment has turned many people into shepherds and lay pastors! Invest specially in leaders and potential pastors and they will grow up to become great ministers!

I have heard people criticizing me for starting churches with people whom they consider not to be pastors. Do not criticize someone who has been holding Shepherds' Camps to train people. Criticize yourself for not having spent hours training your own lay people to be in the ministry.

You must encourage your lay people to become something more than principled citizens of the country. You must encourage them to become soul winners for Jesus. You must want them to be shepherds of God's flock. You must want them to fulfil the Great Commission.

Dear pastor friend, I wrote this book for you! God told me to write it so that you will understand that lay people can and will help you to build your church.

Dear lay person, I wrote this book for you as well! God has a ministry for you. Please do not go to Heaven and discover that you did not even start your ministry before you died! Take what you are reading seriously and learn the art of shepherding and pastoring. Discover for yourself the joy of serving God as a layman.

Chapter 4

Why You Must Share the Burden with Lay People

And the Lord said unto Moses, Gather unto me seventy men of the elders of Israel, whom thou knowest to be the elders of the people, and officers over them; and bring them unto the tabernacle of the congregation, that they may stand there with thee. And I will come down and talk with thee there: and I will take of the spirit which is upon thee, and will put it upon them; and they shall BEAR THE BURDEN of the people with thee, that thou bear it not thyself alone.

Numbers 11:16, 17

One of the most difficult tasks in life is to "lead" people. Moses delivered the Israelites from bondage but struggled to lead them to the Promised Land. They were too difficult for him to handle. Moses' job of leading difficult people is the job that all pastors have to do.

God graciously gave Moses spectacular and sensational miracles. These signs and wonders helped to establish his authority over God's flock. In spite of this, the burden of leading the people was more than he could carry. The Bible calls it a burden - and that is what it is! Moses eventually succumbed to the pressures of leading difficult people and lost his chance to enter the Promised Land.

There Is a Real Burden

If you have a pastor's heart and love people, you cannot disassociate yourself from their problems. Their problems will become your problems and their burdens will affect you!

When God uses you to minister to a large number of people, he expects you to share the burden. Failure to share this burden simply means that you may collapse or come to a standstill in ministry. There are many standstill churches around. They grow to a point but can grow no further. The reason is that they fail to share the burden of ministry.

A balanced church is one that has people of all sorts within it; young, the old, educated and uneducated, rich and poor, and male and female. All these people must be drafted in to the share the burden.

Don't Exclude Anyone

I notice that most churches exclude the educated and the rich from ministry. Usually, the rich are expected to contribute money whilst the educated enhance the image of the church. However, I have found that both the rich and the educated can be spiritually useful.

There are many medical doctors, carpenters, plumbers, specialists, lecturers, architects, and engineers, who serve as lay pastors. These lay pastors share the burden of ministry.

The burden of the ministry cannot be borne by one person. It is simply impossible.

Share the Burden and Have a Larger Church

If you want to have a greater ministry than what you currently have, you must share the burden.

Sometimes people do not share the burden because they want to take all of the glory for themselves. They want people to feel that they are the only ones with a supernatural gift. They want people to show appreciation to them alone.

Others are afraid of rebellion in the camp. How common is the story of associate pastors rebelling. Many senior pastors fear their assistants will outshine them one day. Fear not, only believe! You cannot expand without trusting people. The work is so great that you will never ever be able to do it all alone.

Chapter 5

How Lay People Will Help
to Bring Church Growth

1. **Lay people will help you deal with ungrateful and forgetful sheep.**

   ...in the last days... men shall be... unthankful...

   2 Timothy 3:1, 2

There will always be lay people who are very grateful for your ministry. They will love you and appreciate your efforts for them. These people will help to neutralize the presumption that is common in the congregation. Their grateful speeches will neutralize rebellion in the camp.

You will notice ungratefulness in people by the way they complain. Moses led the Israelites out of bondage and slavery and yet they murmured and complained bitterly against him. Aaron even had to make a golden calf to calm them down.

If something ever goes wrong, you will be surprised at the reactions of people you have ministered to. Many quickly forget what you have done for them.

The things a pastor does are not physically tangible, but spiritual. Many therefore think that the pastor has done nothing for them.

Church members can sin against you after you have been a blessing to them. Don't be shocked! The prophet Jeremiah experienced the same thing from his people. He said, "Shall evil be recompensed for good?..." (Jeremiah 18:20).

The Sin of Hezekiah

Once, a pastor told a very disturbing story. He said that he was surprised when one of his church members came to his house one night to assault him. He couldn't believe that this young man whom he had led to Christ, trained up in the Lord; whose marriage he had blessed and helped through various crises would attack him in that manner.

Dear friend, do not be surprised! Do not expect gratitude from man; expect your rewards from God. Hezekiah was blessed. But he did not "render again". That means he did not show gratitude for all the blessings he had received.

But Hezekiah RENDERED NOT AGAIN according to the benefit done unto him...

2 Chronicles 32:25

This is the nature of man. This is the nature of the people God wants you to lead.

2. Lay people will help you overcome disloyalty in the congregation.

With the help of lay people, you will be able to fight disloyalty in the church. The presence of zealously committed lay workers always inspires more loyalty in the ranks. Lay people, who do not earn money from the church, are a great support to every pastor. Lay people who are loyal will report what is going on in the congregation.

Though Judas walked and ministered with Jesus for three years, he eventually betrayed him for a small amount of money. Betrayal is a part of ministry. It is also a part of life. If you have yet to experience betrayal, I can assure you that you will. The disturbing thing about betrayal is that it comes from people who are supposedly close to you.

You are not greater than your master Jesus! The fact that someone may betray you one day makes it very difficult for you to happily interact and flow with the people. Look closely at the ministry of any great man of God. You will discover that they have all had their fair share of traitors. All of this contributes to the burden and difficulty of ministry.

Yea, mine own familiar friend, in whom I trusted, which did eat of my bread, hath lifted up his heel against me.

Psalm 41:9

Paul experienced sudden desertions by some of his colleagues, like Demas. I remember one young man whom I trained. He was about to take up an important position in the ministry that we had been preparing for, for over a year. On the day he was to fill the position, he suddenly informed me that he was leaving the country. I couldn't believe my ears! All of our months of preparation meant nothing to him. He just abandoned ship without notice. These experiences are all part of the ministry. Abandonment also occurred under the ministry of Apostle Paul.

For Demas hath forsaken me...

2 Timothy 4:10

Because people can abandon you at any time, it is burdensome to lead them.

The presence of committed lay people will always help to share the burden of abandonment. God wants us to be involved in His work. God wants us to be shepherds!

3. **Lay people will help to deal with disrespectful and rebellious church members.**

And Miriam and Aaron spake against Moses ... Hath the Lord indeed spoken only by Moses? HATH HE NOT SPOKEN ALSO BY US?...

Numbers 12:1-2

There are lay people who will sort out disrespectful and rebellious church members for you. You always need people on the ground to deal with church members who make light of pastors. There are people who think their money and status in the secular world gives them a right to say and do anything in the church.

Miriam and Aaron (the closest assistants and closest relatives) spoke against Moses. They most probably said things like, "God also speaks by us" and "Are you the only one God uses?"

22

With time, familiarity creeps in and arrogant people now consider you as an equal. They tend to think, "We can all do it. What's the big deal? You are no different from us!"

This is unfortunate, but real. People easily take you for granted. They murmur and complain against you, forgetting all that you have done for them.

When some church members lose their temper, they will speak to you as though you are a little child.

"You Remind Me of My Father"

One church member approached her pastor after Sunday service. The pastor thought she was about to compliment him for the powerful sermon he had just preached.

She started, "Pastor, you know something? I felt I should tell you that you remind me of my father."

"Oh really?" the pastor responded. He thought he reminded her of some good traits in her father.

She continued, "He was so full of himself and so are you!"

The pastor was taken aback but had to smile and continue as though he had received a compliment. This church member was telling the pastor exactly what she thought of him. Moses also experienced rebels who thought he was "too big" for his shoes. Moses also had people who wanted to cut him down to size. That is why Moses had to share the burden with seventy other elders.

> **Now Korah ... and Dathan ... and Abiram ... and On ... rose up before Moses ... and said ... wherefore then lift ye up yourselves [Moses and Aaron] above the congregation of the Lord?**
>
> **Numbers 16:1-3**

4. **Good lay people encourage others to respond positively to the Word.**

   When any one heareth the word of the kingdom, and UNDERSTANDETH IT NOT...

   Matthew 13:19

The domino effect is when one thing leads to another. When one layperson responds positively to your teaching, others are inspired to do the same. It is always a blessing to have ordinary congregants who are outspoken in their support of you. Sometimes large sections of the congregation do not understand the Word.

Often they do not understand why you have to do fund-raising. Consequently, many do not respond in giving. Many times, I have to explain that they are giving to build a nice church where they can have their weddings, their baby dedications and their ceremonies.

Leading people who have all the above characteristics: ungratefulness, disloyalty, etc., is a major task.

One person cannot do it alone. The burden must be shared with others. Sharing the burden is hard work.

5. Lay people will cause the church to expand by becoming part of the workforce.

The use of lay people as part of the workforce is the secret to unlimited expansion of the church.

Sometimes people think that lay people cannot do much ministry work. Do not be deceived—try using lay people and you will discover how much work they can do.

Lay people can join the pastors to share the burden of the people. Let your lay people know that they are called to share the burden of ministry with you. They will share the burden on earth and they will share the burden of accounting for the sheep in Heaven.

When we established churches in the universities, we entrusted the preaching and pastoring responsibilities to students. I am very proud of these student ministers because of the great job that they have done on the different campuses. I don't have to rush to the different universities every Sunday morning to minister the Word. Ordinary saints have joined in to help. These saints must be perfected (prepared, trained) to do the work of the ministry. Ordinary saints can do the work.

For the perfecting of the saints, for the work of the ministry, for the edifying of the body of Christ:

Ephesians 4:12

The principal strategy for distributing the burden is to involve lay men and women in ministry. No church is capable of employing an endless number of people. Every church has a limit to its resources.

It is not possible to pay salaries and rent an unlimited number of houses for the staff of the ministry. Full-time staff are limited in the amount of work that they can do.

6. Lay people will help you with prayer, visitation, counselling and interaction.

Lay people can help you with the burden of praying, visiting, counselling and interacting with the sheep.

Moses was breaking down under the burden of having to pray, visit, counsel and interact with so many people. God saw a disaster waiting to happen and decided to take of the "spirit" that was on Moses and put it on the seventy leaders "to bear the burden" with him.

And the Lord said unto Moses, Gather unto me SEVENTY MEN of the elders of Israel ... THAT THEY MAY STAND [work] THERE WITH THEE.

Numbers 11:16

Involving students, workers, and professionals helps to distribute the burden to all saints in the church. The Lord wants everyone to be fruitful no matter what they do in life.

7. **Lay people will help you to account for the sheep on the Day of Judgment.**

    ... for they watch for your souls, AS THEY THAT MUST GIVE ACCOUNT, that they may do it with joy...

Hebrews 13:17

The burden of answering for the sheep cannot be borne by one person or a few people who supposedly have a "call". The burden of accounting for hundreds of different people cannot be borne by one person. When I stand before the judgment seat and God asks me about certain souls, I intend to refer to the lay pastors and shepherds I put in charge of these souls.

When the Lord asks me about some souls in the church, I intend to find out who was in charge and tell the Lord to ask that person. I cannot possibly answer for all these different people personally.

Every pastor will have a lot to answer for when he stands before the Lord in Heaven. Your burden is to be able to lead all your sheep to Heaven. Make sure you lose none of them. Every pastor must hope to say, "Of all that you have given me, I have lost none!" Jesus said this phrase in three different places – John 6:39, John 17:12; and John 18:9.

Chapter 6

Five Evils that Evolve When Lay People Are Not Involved in the Ministry

1. **If you do not allow lay people to work in the ministry you will kill the Christian principle of sacrifice in the church.**

    Then said Jesus unto his disciples, If any man will come after me, let him deny himself, and take up his cross, and follow me.

    Matthew 16:24

The symbol of Christianity is the cross. The cross speaks of suffering and dying. God spoke to Abraham and asked him to give up his most treasured possession—his son. Don't listen to anyone who tells you that the day of suffering, sacrificing, losing and dying is over. The day of sacrificing, losing and dying has come. God is requiring us to give up our treasured possessions so that we can serve Him. The church is being filled with people who are not aware that God is calling them to sacrifice. Christianity is a religion of sacrifice. Christianity is based on the cross. Christianity is based on losing your life so that you gain a new life.

Different Sacrifices for Different People

But some people have the mistaken view that God asks everyone to sacrifice their "Isaac". But God did not ask Joseph to sacrifice his sons. Neither did He ask Jacob or Isaac to sacrifice their sons. King David was a man after God's own heart, but God did not ask David to sacrifice his son.

God deals with everyone differently! What God requires of me may be different from what He requires of you. God has asked me for my profession. Perhaps God will not ask you for your profession. But He will ask you for something and you will have to give it up.

Christianity always involves sacrifice. If you do not allow lay people to work in the ministry, they will never learn to give up the smallest things for Christ. If they cannot give up their time, their evenings and their leisure for Christ what will happen if the Lord asks them for their "Isaac"? It is important to expose the lay people in your church to this basic principle of sacrifice.

2. **If you do not allow lay people to work in the ministry you will remove the opportunity for them to demonstrate faithfulness.**

The Bible teaches clearly that he that is faithful with little will be faithful with much.

He that is faithful in that which is least is faithful also in much: and he that is unjust in the least is unjust also in much. If therefore ye have not been faithful in the unrighteous mammon, who will commit to your trust the true riches? And if ye have not been faithful in that which is another man's, who shall give you that which is your own?

Luke 16:10-12

If somebody is not faithful as a layperson, how will he be faithful when he is in full-time ministry?

Many people are not doing well in full-time ministry because they did not do well as lay people.

Did you work for the Lord as a layperson who did not need supervision?

Did you need anybody to tell you to get up to pray?

Did you need anybody to tell you to study your Bible?

Were you faithful when you were in school?

My Lay History

I was a committed worker in the Scripture Union fellowship in my school. I was heavily involved as an organist in a Christian singing group to which I belonged.

I was a drummer and pianist for Victory Church in London.

I was involved with the fellowships in the university. Yet it never once crossed my mind that I should be paid for these things.

This lay ministry is an important background for a future full-time ministry. He that is faithful with lay ministry will be faithful with full-time ministry. Many people who have worked as lay people work even better as full timers.

3. **If you do not allow lay people to work in the ministry you will employ people to do jobs that do not occupy them fully.**

Not every ministry needs a full-time pastor. Many churches can be pastored by unpaid lay pastors.

If there are only twenty-five people in the church, it is obvious that it cannot sustain and does not need a full-time minister. Many of the church members secretly ask, "What does the full-time pastor do all day?"

Many people think that pastors sleep from morning to evening. The fact is that there isn't so much to do with a congregation of thirty. The ministry has to develop to the point where it needs a full-time worker. The other reality is that most of the members are at work during the day and only become available in the evenings.

Pastors are not bankers, accountants or pharmacists. They are shepherds who are supposed to look after sheep. Working hours are different for different professions! I do not work from nine to five everyday because I am not an accountant. I am a pastor! When the sheep become available in the evenings I become very active. That is why I work late into the night.

Some pastors become idle and lazy as they wait for Sunday when they can deliver their next sermon.

For we hear that there are some which walk among you disorderly, WORKING NOT AT ALL...

2 Thessalonians 3:11

Let us be honest! Let us be realistic! Does your church need so many full-time pastors? Does it need even one full-time pastor? Can the income of the church sustain the pastor and his family? Can the pastor not find a secular job to do? Pastors are frustrated and fearful because they are not sure whether they will be able to survive until the next month.

You can overcome that frustration today! Get a job and pastor the church on the side until it grows and demands your full attention!

The Swiss missionaries who were sent to Ghana many years ago were sent as self-sustaining ministers. They came equipped with skills that would enable them to work in Africa as they did their ministry work. That is a good example to follow. We need self-sustaining ministers today more than ever before. Most churches cannot bear the burden of maintaining so many full-time pastors.

You must keep your ministry staff as small as possible so that you can pay them properly. You must not have idle and discontented people around you. Idleness leads to laziness and laziness leads to discontentment and discontentment leads to disloyalty.

And withal they learn to be idle, wandering about from house to house; and not only idle, but tattlers also and busybodies, speaking things which they ought not.
1 Timothy 5:13

4. If you do not allow lay people to work in the ministry everything done in the church will be related to money.

He that loveth silver shall not be satisfied with silver; nor he that loveth abundance with increase: this is also vanity.
Ecclesiastes 5:10

The ministry is not an alternative source of employment for anyone. It was never intended to be! It is a special job that God gives to those whom He has called. **As the church becomes**

larger, it often deteriorates into a source of employment for the unemployed. This attracts many people who have no better options. What happens to the church? It becomes full of seekers of wealth and lovers of silver. The church is filled with pastors who constantly fight for better salaries and conditions of service.

I Never Knew Anyone Earned Money for Preaching

I started ministry as a layperson, so the idea of being paid in full-time ministry came up much later. I started my church as a medical student and found myself pastoring while at the same time practising medicine. Later on, I went into business and combined it with pastoral work.

At the end of 1990, the Lord told me to leave everything I was doing and enter into full-time ministry. It was not an easy decision for me. Since January 1st, 1991 I have been full-time in the ministry for the Lord Jesus.

There are many people who are in full-time ministry who should not really be there. There are many people who I believe should find secular jobs! How can a church with sixty members sustain eight full-time pastors and their families? Yet, this is the case in many ministries. Success in the ministry requires both power and wisdom.

But unto them which are called, both Jews and Greeks, Christ the power of God, and the wisdom of God.

1 Corinthians 1:24

Many pastors see the ministry as a way to travel around the world and to drive nice cars. I did not enter the ministry in order to drive a nice car. I do drive a nice car now but I did not come into the ministry because I wanted to have the nice things of this world. In fact, coming into full-time ministry was, for me, the end of all hopes of ever having the nice things of this world.

Yea doubtless, and I count all things but loss for the excellency of the knowledge of Christ Jesus my Lord: for whom I HAVE SUFFERED THE LOSS OF ALL

THINGS, and do count them but dung, that I may win Christ,

Philippians 3:8

A minister who is going to serve God properly must have died to the love for silver and gold. Why is this? The Bible teaches that those that love silver are never satisfied with silver. The more you give them, the more they want. Why is it that the richest people in this world are often the biggest thieves?

Is it because they are poor? Is it because they are in need? Certainly not! It is because of the greed for more and more and more!

You cannot satisfy people with more and more money. From experience, whenever I have felt under pressure to raise salaries, I have often discovered it does not solve the problem!

Senior pastors, if you feel under pressure to raise salaries and give more and more benefits, you will discover that the problem never goes away. Full-time ministers must be people who just want to serve the Lord at heart. This does not mean that people will be poor but it means that the heart is not craving endlessly after more and more.

Soon the church becomes unionized with the workers against the management, and the management against the workers! The "management" are often the senior pastors who make decisions and the "workers" are the other pastors and workers who are not involved in the decision-making. You should see the bitterness, petty jealousies and bickering amongst the full-time staff of many churches and ministries. This often extends to their families and pastor's wives pick up quarrels with other pastor's wives.

I would rather have one or two workers with peace than to have a hundred unhappy and discontented full-time staff.

5. **If you do not allow lay people to work in the ministry they will not learn the importance of obedience and submission.**

As you enter into full-time ministry you must be open for whatever the future will bring. You may be rich or you may be poor. You may have abundance or you may live in the "want of all things". Are you ready for anything?

Verily, verily, I say unto thee, When thou wast young, thou girdedst thyself, and walkedst whither thou wouldest: but when thou shalt be old, thou shalt stretch forth thy hands, and another shall gird thee, and carry thee whither thou wouldest not. This spake he, signifying by what death he should glorify God. And when he had spoken this, he saith unto him, Follow me.
John 21:18-19

Jesus told Peter to be ready for anything. Be ready to be carried anywhere. It will no longer be your will, but God's will. You are not the commander, you are just one of God's workers. One of the reasons why I am in the ministry is because I have no choice.

...woe is unto me, if I preach not the gospel!
1 Corinthians 9:16

There are detractors, faultfinders, analysts and commentators who talk about me all the time. I have no time for empty chatter. I prefer to hear my dogs barking in the morning than to listen to their hateful and sarcastic comments. I must continue doing what God has called me to do. Some people love me for what I do and others hate me. I thank God for them all. But I press on for the mark of the prize of the high calling.

I am totally surrendered to fulfilling the call of God upon my life, so help me God!

Section 3

CHURCH GROWTH AND PASTORAL TECHNIQUES

Chapter 7

The Art of Wielding a
Rod and a Staff

The Equipment of a Shepherd

. . . thy ROD and thy STAFF they comfort me.
Psalm 23:1, 4

Without the ability to use your equipment you cannot achieve church growth. A shepherd must know how to use his rod and his staff. The equipment of a good shepherd are his rod and his staff. Indeed, every profession has its tools.

Guns are the equipment of soldiers with which they kill and destroy.

The stethoscope is one of the key tools of a doctor.

How to Use Your Rod and Your Staff

1. **The rod and staff are used to lead and to rule.**

   And out of his mouth goeth a sharp sword ... and he shall rule them with a ROD OF IRON...
   Revelation 19:15

   You must learn to wield the rod and the staff as tools for ruling. The traditional perception of a pastor is of someone who is soft, kind-hearted, compassionate, poorly paid, available at all times, and a never-complaining doormat. This is not a picture of a ruler but rather a picture of one who is ruled. I believe that a pastor must be kind-hearted and patient, but one of his cardinal roles is to lead and to rule. A pastor is the head of the local church. A head must take decisions.

The Lord is my shepherd... HE LEADETH ME beside the still waters.

Psalm 23:1, 2

A true shepherd leads sheep to the place where they need to go. You cannot be a good leader if you are weak. Every church needs a strong voice that is confident and bold in the Lord. The sheep are looking for someone with direction, who knows where he is going. A pastor must lead the people spiritually and in other areas such as in the family and social dimensions.

When the church does not have a strong capable leader, something is wrong.

Learn to speak to your sheep with authority. I do not mean you should dominate their lives. Lead them with a high level of confidence and control. Sheep are meant to be led.

You have authority over the sheep God has placed in your care. You will answer for their souls one day.

A leader who refuses to take important decisions is doomed to failure.

A good leader takes decisions when all necessary information has come to him! These decisions may be hard and painful. If you, as the shepherd do not take them, your church is doomed to wither.

Just look around and see how many churches are dead and lifeless. They are a far cry from what their founders had envisaged. This is because as wrong things began to creep in, the leaders were afraid to rock the boat and take important decisions.

Sometimes when I look at some hopelessly incompetent government corporations and agencies, I just marvel. They make huge losses, and generate a lot of waste in the system. I have been to government offices where I see everyone reading newspapers. Sometimes you see twenty secretaries in one office with one typewriter. They have nothing to do, yet they are paid with the taxpayers' money every month. What a pity! They sleep, eat and chat all day. Their managers are afraid to take the decision that nineteen out of the twenty typists must be laid off.

The country becomes poorer and poorer and people wonder why. The reason is simple. The leaders have refused to assess the situation and take a strong but hard decision. They are refusing to rule. The fear of losing political power makes democratic leaders become liars and hypocrites.

I am not afraid of taking such decisions because I realize that the church will deteriorate if I do not.

Remove stagnating leaders and replace them with willing and capable workers. I make the necessary changes in my staff and with my lay pastors when I realize a change must be made.

Don't be afraid of changes. Sometimes, it is only a big change that will lead to a big breakthrough. **A minor change will take place when you take minor decisions. But a major transformation will occur when you are bold enough to take a major decision.** Be a strong ruler and lead your sheep to green pastures.

Lady pastors can learn to be strong firm leaders without being ill-natured and quarrelsome. Lady shepherds should be gentle and effective, without being cantankerous.

2. The rod and staff are used for a way-making ministry.

And the Lord said unto Moses ... But LIFT THOU UP THY ROD, and stretch out thine hand over the sea, and divide it: and the children of Israel shall go on dry ground through the midst of the sea.
Exodus 14:15, 16

You must learn to wield the rod and the staff as tools for making a way. As a leader, God will tell you to speak to His people, giving them many instructions. After you have given instructions to the sheep, you must help them to obey the Word. A true shepherd loves his sheep and tries to help them to obey God.

Moses was the shepherd of the people of Israel. His instructions were to cross the Red Sea. After receiving that command he stretched forth his rod and made a way where there was no way. That is what I call the way-making ministry of the pastor.

Every full-time minister or lay pastor must learn to make a way where there seems to be no way for the people of God.

When some of your sheep think that their house is too far away from the church, go and visit them wherever they live. This will prove to them that their homes are not too far.

My Visit Produced a Pastor

I knew a family that lived about a two-hour train ride from one of our churches. When I called them, they said it was too far to attend church. So one Saturday, I took a car and together with another pastor, we drove all the way to their house. They were so surprised to see us visiting them.

This is one thing that visits do. It establishes the fact that people are not too far away. From that day, the entire family decided to come to church, taking the train and travelling two hours to church.

They did this for a number of years, and today one of them is a pastor. Make a way for your sheep. Help them to see that it is possible to obey the Word of God. Sometimes when they don't have money, give them some money to help them attend. You may not be able to give them money all the time, but the fact that you did it once or twice encourages them and shows that you really care. This is the pastor's heart.

Make a Way for Your Sheep to Get Married

As a pastor, it is easy to see that your sheep are looking for husbands or wives. Don't just look on unconcerned and preach about how good it is to be married. Discuss the practical issues of choosing a partner with them. Help them to notice one another. That is what we call "Shepherdorial Linking."

Teach your members that they can find a good partner within the church. Some people may not like that idea, but it works and it stabilizes the sheep. Of course, do not force people to marry each other.

You must warn them that happiness is not guaranteed just because they marry a person you recommended. This is because marriage is complex and you don't want anyone cursing you for the rest of their lives.

Make a Way for Sheep to Find Jobs

I preach to my members about prosperity. After I've done that, the way-making anointing comes upon me and I help them to get jobs. If one of my church members is strategically positioned as an employer, I would speak to them about a sheep who needs employment.

Sometimes a person you have recommended will disgrace you. But do not let that deter you from making a way for other good sheep.

It is not good enough to say "Cross the Red Sea"; you must make a way for them to cross!

Make a Way for Your Sheep to Attend Programmes in Church

I have often changed meeting times or rehearsal times so that one person could attend. I am a pastor and I want all of my sheep to attend the meetings. Schedule reasonable meeting times. *Make things possible for people.* That is the way-making ministry in action.

Schedule fewer meeting times without compromising the number of meetings. Sunday is a good time to meet and counsel your sheep. You can always combine meetings. Don't let people travel to church twice when they could have come once.

Be an expert at overcoming the excuses of church members. When they say that church services are too long, point out to them how many hours they spend watching television. When they say that the church is too far from their homes, ask them how far their jobs are from their homes. When the church member doesn't have shoes, get him a pair. Be a way-maker. Be like Moses. Make a way through the Red Sea with your rod and your staff.

3. The rod and the staff are used for taking territories in ministry.

You must learn to wield the rod and the staff as tools for taking territories. If you have a burning vision for a mega church you will always want to take more territory for Christ. **You can take more territory for God through prayer and fasting.** You can lead your people into spiritual warfare.

I always have a new vision for my church. When I had twenty members, I had a vision to have fifty. When I had fifty people at the Korle Bu Teaching Hospital, I dreamed of the day when I would see a hundred people sitting in church on Sunday morning.

When I had five hundred, I dreamt of a thousand. Mega Church Pastor, you must have dreams for greater territories for the kingdom of God. We are not a social club. We are not fighting a psychological warfare. We are into spiritual warfare.

And Moses said unto Joshua, Choose us out men, and go out, fight with Amalek: tomorrow I will stand on the top of the hill with the ROD OF GOD in mine hand. And it came to pass, when Moses held up his hand, that Israel prevailed: and when he let down his hand, Amalek prevailed.

Exodus 17:9, 11

People who take new territories are people who fast and pray. I believe in praying for long periods. I believe in fasting as the Spirit leads. Moses, the shepherd of God's people, stretched out his rod in warfare against Amalek. Moses' rod symbolized the power of intercessory prayer. It is the art of travailing in prayer for the ministry.

What you see happening in the physical is only a manifestation of what has taken place in the spiritual realm.

Anyone who calls himself a pastor must learn to fight with prayer in the realm of the spirit. If you want to have a big church, you must learn to fight for it in the spiritual realm. Every territory is occupied by evil spirits who dominate the area.

When I travel from place to place, I can virtually feel the difference in the spiritual atmosphere. When I am in Ghana, I sense a lighter and easier spiritual climate. When I am in Germany I sense the presence of many marauding evil spirits.

Develop the art of intercession for taking more territories for God. That means you must develop several important prayer skills.

4.   The rod and staff are used to comfort people.

...thy rod and thy staff they comfort me.

Psalm 23:4

You must learn to wield the rod and the staff as tools for comforting the sheep. One of the principal ministries of a shepherd is to comfort the sheep. Every sheep should be able to say to his shepherd, "Your rod and your staff comfort me." Some people do not know why their churches do not grow.

The shepherd must genuinely love the sheep and care for them when they are in trouble. Never lose the opportunity to be by your sheep's side in their time of difficulty. The duty of the lay pastor is to stand by his sheep in the time of their greatest need and greatest joy. It is not an option! Remember that, sorrow shared is half sorrow, and joy shared is double joy. The sheep want to share their sorrows and their joys with their pastor.

It is the duty of the shepherd to comfort the sheep. The comforting ministry starts by showing interest in things that are important to the sheep. Be interested in all of their major events; especially the birth of a child, marriages, sickness and funerals. God expects you to be there!

What is important to your sheep must be important to you. If you claim to be a pastor, what are you doing to show real love to your sheep?

Shepherds, if you genuinely do not love your people, they will not respond to your good preaching. The Bible says that God is angry with the shepherds because they have not ministered to the sheep under the comforting ministry.

The diseased have ye not strengthened, neither have ye healed that which was sick, neither have ye bound up that which was broken, neither have ye brought again that which was driven away, neither have ye sought that which was lost; but with force and with cruelty have ye ruled them.

Ezekiel 34:4

The sheep often know the Word before you preach. What they want is some love. Everybody responds to love. It is only demons that cannot be loved! Remember that love never fails. The Bible does not say, "Preaching never fails" or, "Teaching never fails". The Bible says, "Love never fails". The comforting ministry is love in action.

5. The rod and staff are used for self-assessment.

One of the principal duties of a shepherd is to do what I call measuring the temple. Measuring the temple helps you to know where you stand.

And there was given me a reed like unto a rod: and the angel stood, saying, Rise, and MEASURE the temple of God, and the altar, and them that worship therein.

Revelation 11:1

This involves a critical analysis of the way things are going. Pastors need to take time off to analyze themselves and to see whether things are being done according to the vision that God gave.

You must constantly measure yourself. Ask yourself, "Am I doing what God called me to do?" The reason why I am writing books now is because I believe it is in obedience to God. No matter what I do, I am constantly trying to fulfil the specific call of God on my life.

Only Twenty-five Members after Twelve Years

I was chatting with a pastor who had been in the ministry for twelve years. After being in the ministry for twelve years, he only had twenty-five members in his church. His church was in a city where there were many large churches.

After many years of hard work there was little growth. Anything that is alive and healthy grows. If this pastor were to have analyzed his ministry properly, he would have come up with some important decisions.

For instance, he may have realized that he was better suited to be an assistant than to be a head.

Perhaps he would have discovered that he lacked a genuine call of God.

Perhaps he would have realized how he needed to close down the church. Analysis and self-assessment are very important in ministry. They help you to make vital mid-stream corrections.

He Returned to the Ministry

Some years ago, I spoke to a pastor friend of mine. I had known this pastor for several years. He had been actively pastoring a church in a large city.

Due to circumstances beyond his control, he found himself in another city. There he just attended a dead church. He was no longer actively involved in the ministry. He was just a church attendee.

I spoke to him and said, "If you are called of God to the ministry, then wherever you are and whatever your circumstances are you must fulfil your ministry." I impressed upon him to analyze his condition (measuring ministry) as a pastor and take the important decisions that would bring him to a place where he was fulfilling his divine call. I'm happy to say that he did. Today, he is overseeing many churches.

EXAMINE YOURSELVES, whether ye be in the faith; prove your own selves...

2 Corinthians 13:5

Examine yourselves to see whether you are within your call and whether there is anything that you have to change.

Can you imagine if the Mercedes-Benz car that is being sold today is exactly the same as it was fifty years ago? Can you imagine what it would be like if these car makers were to carry on for years without making changes? But that is how many churches are. They carry on for years without trying to make improvements

Our churches and ministries must be - continually upgraded and improved.

We must compare what we are doing to what is in the Bible. If you see something in the Bible that is not in your church, strive to attain that biblical standard.

I always marvel at people who fight against miracles and prophecies. Prophecies and prophets are in the Bible. The entire Bible is full of testimonies of supernatural and spectacular miracles.

If you have no miracles in your church, please do not say that the day of miracles has passed.

Just work on yourself until you have the miraculous operating in your ministry.

Accept the fact that there are biblical standards to attain! It is because we don't measure what we are doing, that we continue in the wrong thing for a long time.

Ask yourselves, "Am I a good person?" Ask your wife or husband what she/he thinks about you. Ask yourself, "How many people should there be in the church at this stage?" Measure your performance and analyze your duties! If you assess yourself, God will not have to judge you.

But he that is spiritual judgeth all things, yet he himself is judged of no man.

1 Corinthians 2:15

6. The rod and staff are used in correcting people.

...SHALL I COME UNTO YOU WITH A ROD, or in love, and in the spirit of meekness?

1 Corinthians 4:21

You must learn to wield the rod and the staff as tools to correct people. Some people do not like it when the pastor points out evil and corrects it. The worst type of pastor is the one who cannot correct things that are going out of line. It is important to purge out certain things from the flock. When your sheep realize that you are a weak leader, they will take you for a ride.

Black Beauty

Many years ago, I went for a ride on a horse called Black Beauty. This was at Burma Camp, a military riding school in the city of Accra. I was a new rider and the horse soon realized that I was a novice. Our instructor was taking us on a ride through various fields in the countryside.

When we got to the boundary of the riding school, the horse didn't feel like going out for the ride so it stopped at the gate. I had a whip in my hand so I hit the horse several times and it began to kick and jump.

Soon, it knew that I was afraid of it. Some of the more experienced riders in the group came alongside and encouraged me to control my horse and bring it out into the field.

Would you believe that the horse calmly turned around and took me back to its stable? It utterly refused to go out on a ride that afternoon. I would say that the horse rode me; I didn't ride it!

Some months later after I became experienced, this horse was no match for me. I could make it do anything I wanted it to do.

That is how the pastor must be with the sheep. If the people you are leading feel that you are weak, they will lead you. When they realize that you are strong, they will stay in line.

Identify disloyal people and remove them from the fold. Rebuke people publicly when you have to.

Strength to Drive out Thieves

One Tuesday night, during a church service, my associate pastor invited a church member to come up on stage. This young man was notorious for stealing.

The associate pastor announced to the church that the young man was a dangerous thief who was going about taking things from church members. He went on to say that everybody in the church should be careful of him and not believe his lies anymore.

The church was dead calm for a second and then suddenly burst out in thunderous applause. The young man had thought that he could take us for granted. He thought that because we were a church we would allow him to do anything he wanted. That was his mistake and the sheep appreciated the strong leadership of the pastor.

...Know ye not that a little leaven leaventh the whole lump? Purge out therefore the old leaven...
1 Corinthians 5:6, 7

To some of the sheep, you must be gentle and say things like:

"I am disappointed in you."
"I wasn't expecting this from you."
"I was expecting something better from you."
"Let this never happen again."
"Shame."
"I give you 20% for your Christianity."

And of some have compassion, making a difference:
Jude 22

Correcting the sheep does not mean you should disgrace them. You can correct them without disgracing them. If you do not correct them, that thing will begin to spread among the congregation.

The "Ruby, Walk Out!" (RWO) Treatment

To some of the sheep, you must be rough and hard. With others, you must actually dismiss them from the church. I remember one pastor who stood in the pulpit and looked at two giggling girls and shouted from the pulpit, "Ruby, Walk Out!" She had no choice but to walk out, never to return.

Cast out the scorner, and contention shall go out; yea, strife and reproach shall cease.
Proverbs 22:10

I call this the RWO treatment. Some people need to be dismissed from the church. Their presence in the church is not desirable or helpful, so get rid of them. It's as simple as that!

7. The rod and staff are used to feed the sheep.

You must learn to wield the rod and the staff as tools for feeding the sheep. It is a principal duty of a shepherd to feed his sheep. Everything else comes after he has done this principal duty. The authority to lead is given to those with the ability to feed.

FEED THY PEOPLE WITH THY ROD, the flock of thine heritage, which dwell solitarily in the wood, in the midst of Carmel: let them feed in Bashan and Gilead, as in the days of old.
Micah 7:14

I have people in my church who are older and wiser than I am in many respects. Yet in the church, I am their leader and

I minister to them. Where would I get the authority to advise someone who could be my father or my mother? This authority is found in the ability to feed.

Where does your earthly father get his authority from? It comes from the fact that he has fed you for years and continues to feed you. When your parents no longer feed you, the authority they have over your life reduces.

Jesus said to Peter three times, "Feed my sheep". It is very important to the Lord that His sheep are well fed on the Word of God.

...Jesus saith unto him, Feed my sheep.

John 21:17

The principal duty of all ministry offices is to preach and to teach the Word of God.

And Jesus went about all the cities and villages, TEACHING in their synagogues, and PREACHING the gospel of the kingdom...

Matthew 9:35

Paul was an apostle and a prophet. He called himself an apostle to the Gentiles.

Paul, AN APOSTLE of Jesus Christ by the will of God...

2 Timothy 1:1

Paul went on to say in verse eleven,

Whereunto I am appointed a PREACHER, and an apostle, and a TEACHER of the Gentiles.

2 Timothy 1:11

It should be clear to every minister that our main resolve is to preach and teach the Word. What did Paul tell Timothy?

I charge thee therefore before God, and the Lord Jesus Christ...PREACH THE WORD...

2 Timothy 4:1, 2

Paul predicted that a time would come when people would not want the Bible to be preached.

For the time will come when they will not endure sound doctrine; but after their own lusts they shall heap to themselves teachers, having itching ears; And they shall turn away their ears from the truth, and shall be turned unto fables.

2 Timothy 4:3, 4

I believe that time has come now! Many prefer to be prophesied to. They want a quick, "bless me" prayer and some anointing with oil.

Pastors, develop your ability to feed and to preach. It is your one great asset. Look around you and observe the great men of God you know. You will discover that every one of them has a strong ability to preach and to teach.

Chapter 8

Shepherding Techniques that Lead to Church Growth

Jesus Christ was many things to us. He called Himself different things at different times. At one time He said He was the way, the truth and the life. He announced that He was the door. He declared that He was the bread of life and the light of the world.

But He also said He was the good shepherd.

What did Jesus mean when He said He was a good shepherd? The word shepherd in John 10:11 is translated from the Greek word poimen. It is this same word, poimen, which is translated pastor in Ephesians 4:11.

And he gave some, apostles; and some, prophets; and some, evangelists; and some, pastors [poimen] and teachers;

Ephesians 4:11

The word shepherd is interchangeable with the word pastor. What the Lord was really saying was, "I am the good pastor". Throughout the Bible, Jesus referred to Himself as a shepherd or a pastor.

Jesus said He was a good shepherd. What techniques did He use? He spoke extensively about the techniques of a good shepherd in the tenth chapter of John. What were His techniques? What were His methods? Below are the techniques that made Jesus a good shepherd.

1. **A good shepherding technique is to be ahead of your sheep.**

    To him the porter openeth...and LEADETH THEM OUT.

    John 10:3

What does it mean to lead sheep? It means to be practically available for them to see and learn from you in every area of life and ministry. Anything you want your sheep to do, you must first do it yourself. They will follow you if they see you doing it first!

A pastor who wants his church members to pray must practically lead them into prayer. When the sheep see the shepherd taking the lead, they are convinced that the ground is safe. A bad shepherd will sit at home and send the members to go for a prayer meeting alone.

In our church, I have always tried to do first, what I wanted my people to do. When we were building a basement in our church, we could not afford to hire the necessary machinery. We had to dig ourselves. I needed the help of the entire church to drill and dig very deep into the ground. After that, we needed to carry tons of red sand out of the pit.

I could have easily delegated the digging to some others, but I decided to dig and carry the sand myself. My decision motivated members of all social standings to get involved.

University students, lawyers, doctors and businessmen all joined in to work. They worked with all their might. Why was that? They had seen their shepherd taking the lead.

Notice what made David popular.

But all Israel and Judah loved David, because he went out and came in before them.
1 Samuel 18:16

Why did the subjects of Israel love David? The answer is simple. They could see him practically going in and out with them. They saw him doing things with them.

Sometimes we have long periods of fasting with all-night prayer meetings everyday. You would be surprised to see how many people attend every night. I tell my members that I am struggling and suffering in the fast just like them, and they love to hear how I am suffering too. The sheep are always happy to identify with the shepherd when the shepherd identifies with them.

Leadership is very spiritual. Even when people do not see you physically, they follow you spiritually. Sheep have a mysterious way of becoming like their shepherd. They are following him in the Spirit.

Go ahead of your sheep. Do not operate as a super executive, just walking in and out like a "big shot". There is no place for "big shots" in the harvest field. There is no place for "unreal leaders" in the real world of the sheep.

2. **A good shepherding technique is to know your sheep by their names.**

   ...and he calleth his own sheep by NAME...
   John 10:3

   You must know the names of your sheep. You must want to know all their names and call them by name. Nobody is a number! Nobody wants to be called "Hey!" or "You there!"

   You must get to know new people everyday. Keep asking their names until the name sticks. I am not ashamed of asking somebody his name seven times until it sticks. When you know the sheep by name an important spiritual attachment is formed.

3. **A good shepherding technique is to let your voice be known by the sheep.**

   ...for they know his voice. And a stranger will they not follow...
   John 10:4-5

   How do people know the voice of the shepherd? How do you know the voice of someone? It is because you have heard them speak to you time and time again. A good shepherd must speak to his sheep over and over until they know his voice.

   I preach to my church all the time. I do not often have guest speakers. I believe in guest speakers, but I believe the best person to preach to my sheep is me because I am their shepherd.

When a woman gives birth to a baby, her breasts are full of milk for the new child. So it is with the shepherd. His spirit is full of the Word to give to his children. No other woman's body and breasts are better qualified to feed her own child. Nature made it that way. Because you gave birth, you are naturally primed up to feed what you have brought forth.

When your sheep are used to your voice, they will not follow strangers. If you call yourself a pastor, rise-up and feed your sheep regularly. Preach to them all of the time, and teach them from your heart. They will grow up and give birth to others.

They will know your voice on the issues of marriage, business, success and life in general. They will only want to hear your voice concerning different aspects of their lives. The voice of a true shepherd always rings in the spirit of his sheep. I question whether you are a real shepherd if you do not regularly and consistently feed your sheep.

4.   A good shepherding technique is to stay with the sheep.

The hireling fleeth, because he is an hireling, and careth not for the sheep.

John 10:13

Anyone who calls himself a pastor will want to stay around and mingle with the members, talk with them and be interested in them. David said,

One thing have I desired of the Lord, that will I seek after; THAT I MAY DWELL IN THE HOUSE OF THE LORD all the days of my life, to behold the beauty of the Lord, and to inquire in his temple.

Psalm 27:4

David wanted to stay in the house of the Lord. He actually wanted to live there. And you want to rush home! Are you really called?

I question the genuineness of a pastor who has no interest in staying around after service to mingle and chat with the sheep.

The Bible says that the hireling flees. This means that he dashes off quickly! He wants to get away from the people!

Such people cannot stand visitors in their homes. They always say things like, "I need my privacy, I need my space" or "I can't stand having all these people around" and "I can't cook for so many people". Remember that a bishop is supposed to be "given to hospitality" (1Timothy 3:2).

5. A good shepherding technique is to know your sheep.

I am the good shepherd, and know my sheep, and am known of mine.

John 10:14

Knowing your sheep means that you must know their names, where they live and where they work. You know about their health, their friends, and their school. You know when they are writing exams. You know their family, their spouses and who they live with.

You must know their financial situation and their occupation. Simply know all aspects of their lives. Know means know! It is only when you know more details about your sheep that you can help or advise them properly.

I once asked a pastor about one of his sheep. I asked, "Is he married?"

He answered, "I don't know."

"Where does he work?"

"I'm not sure." He answered.

"Did he come to church last week?"

"I didn't see him," he replied.

In a very large church, you may excuse the pastor if he does not know these details. But in a small community church, the pastor has no excuse when he does not know the details about his sheep.

Brother X, Pastor X

I remember a pastor in my church who used to belong to another church. One day, at a wedding, he happened to meet his former senior pastor. His senior pastor said to him, "Brother 'X', it is a long time since I saw you."

"Did you come to church last Sunday?" the senior pastor asked.

Brother 'X' (who had now become a pastor in my church) smiled and said, "No pastor I didn't."

This senior pastor did not know that this brother had long stopped attending his church. He did not know that this gentleman had even become a pastor in another ministry. How sad!

Jesus said that a good pastor knows his sheep. If God gives you twenty people to look after, make sure you know all about them. Do not let any of them slip out of your hands. Jesus kept saying, "Those that thou gavest me I have kept, and none of them is lost." (John 17:12). It is important to have many junior pastors and shepherds to work with the senior pastor so that none of the sheep get lost.

God will hold us accountable for every single sheep that is lost. Keep the sheep that God has given to you.

6. A good shepherding technique is to be known by the sheep.

A good shepherd "opens up" his life to the sheep so that they can know about him. The sheep are interested in the shepherd's life. Do not be a mystery figure to your sheep. Let them know how real you are and how you experience the same problems and temptations they do.

7. A good shepherding technique is to keep the church family together.

One of the cardinal features of the pastoral calling is the ability to keep many people together throughout the years.

The longer a group of people stay together the more the people step on each other's toes. The conflicts of a family begin to rise. Brothers turn against brothers and sisters against sisters.

It is a good pastor who keeps everybody together. The pastoral gift keeps employers in the same church with employees. The anointing on the shepherd is able to keep the old in the same room with the young. It keeps the married flowing with the unmarried.

As the church grows, good shepherding techniques will keep enemies worshipping together under the same roof.

It is good shepherding techniques that will keep debtors and creditors within the same fold and prevent them from tearing each other apart.

But he that is an hireling, and not the shepherd, whose own the sheep are not, seeth the wolf coming, and leaveth the sheep, and fleeth: and the wolf catcheth them, and SCATTERETH THE SHEEP.

John 10:12

8. A good shepherding technique is to notice the problems of your sheep.

But he that is an hireling, and not a shepherd, whose own the sheep are not, SEETH THE WOLF COMING...

John 10:12

The Scripture tells us that the good shepherd can see the wolf coming. He sees the problems of his people and is concerned. He knows when they are doing exams. He knows when they are having marital problems.

He knows when their businesses are going through "tough times". When a sheep fails his exams or loses a loved one, a wolf of discouragement and frustration is soon to come. A good shepherd must be able to see the wolf and move into action.

The bad shepherd sees the wolves but says, "That's your problem!" The good pastor will always notice when the sheep are in trouble.

56

9. **A good shepherding technique is to deliver your sheep from captivity.**

    ...and the wolf catcheth them, and scattereth the sheep.

    John 10:12

Pastors, rise up and pray for your sheep! Minister to their needs. Apart from preaching, pray for their deliverance from witchcraft, demons and diseases. People love to be prayed for by their pastor. Pray for them, anointing them with oil. They need this encouragement and ministration.

10. **A good shepherding technique is to give your life for the work of God.**

    I am the good shepherd: the good shepherd giveth his life for the sheep.

    John 10:11

A good shepherd sacrifices his life for the sheep. The bad shepherd is only prepared to give two hours of his time on Sundays. He always wants to get away from the crowd.

If a woman desires to be a good wife, she must give herself fully to her husband. If you want to be a good doctor, you must give yourself fully to medicine. Similarly, if you want to be a good shepherd, you must give your life and your time to the high calling of the pastoral office. It is worth it at the end of the day.

Decide to use the best shepherding techniques. Give yourself fully to this work. You will soon have a mega church.

Section 4

CHURCH GROWTH AND THE WISE MANAGEMENT OF MONEY

Chapter 9

How Wise Management of Church Money Can Lead to Church Growth

Your handling of the church's money will greatly affect church growth. Your handling of the church's money will cause the people to have faith in you or to lose confidence in you. In other words, the congregation will judge you by the way you handle the offerings they entrusted to you. As they see their donations being put to good use, their commitment will rise. They will see you as a wise leader because you used the money carefully. It is important that the church members see you as a wise person rather than as a fool. If they see you as a wise person, they will entrust more money to your care.

Almost every strategy for church growth will require the use of money. You will need money to organize camps and conventions. You will need money to go on the radio and television. You will need money to do outreaches, crusades and breakfast meetings. Without a good supply of money most of your dreams and visions will die in your belly.

Keys to Handling the Money

1. **Managing money involves a lot of wisdom.** It is important to use secular principles to manage the money of your church.

2. **Over-spiritualizing financial issues is the number one cause for the financial confusion that plagues churches.**

3. **Church employees must pay taxes**. The church itself does not pay tax. However, individuals who work for the church must pay tax. If a church engages in any kind of business or profit-making activity, it must pay taxes on the income made from that.

In other words, churches do not pay taxes on the tithe, offerings and gifts received. However, tax should be paid from income generated from farms, shops and other businesses. Do not spiritualize the paying of tax.

4. **Avoid debt.** Although this instruction sounds simple, it is probably the most profound piece of advice I could give to any ministry. Debts have closed down many churches. Debts have deceived many pastors into a false sense of prosperity. Debts have deceived pastors into over-extending themselves. Many borrow until they cross the threshold where they have borrowed too much. You can prosper without borrowing money.

5. **Employ wisely and carefully.** The more people you employ, the more salaries you have to pay. As the saying goes, "the fewer the merrier". It is possible to do many things with a few employees. It is possible to accomplish much with fewer but better qualified people.

6. **There is nothing prestigious about having many employees in your ministry.** God did not call you to create jobs. He called you to win souls.

7. **Start a building project as early as possible.** As soon as your church begins a building project, your finances will improve and you will be surprised at what you are able to accomplish. Do not wait to see huge sums of money before you begin a building project. The building project you embark upon will be the greatest evidence of the financial integrity of your ministry.

8. **Do not start a grandiose project that is far bigger than your ministry.** You may never finish it and your church members may be discouraged by the unending nature of your building project.

9. **There are many huge building projects which are impressive to men but which God did not initiate.** Unfortunately, many of these grandiose projects are empty

or half-filled shortly after completion. Some churches are only filled on the day of their dedication.

10. **Grandiose building projects inflict great stresses on the senior pastor.** These stressed-out pastors tend to preach mostly about finances because there is a great and pressing need for money.

11. **Meet the needs of the church before you meet the needs of the pastor.** For instance, put up a building for the church before you build a mansion for the senior pastor. Seeing their church building come up generates much confidence and inspires the church members to give.

12. **Church members may encourage the pastor to buy the nicest car for himself.** Many members have mixed feelings about their pastor's prosperity! On one hand, they are happy that he is doing well, but on the other hand, they wonder whether money is being used wisely.

13. **Since you cannot always explain the source of all your blessings as a pastor, do not openly display everything you have.**

14. **Separate the Pastor's money from the church's money.**

    1. It is important to differentiate between the money of the church and the pastor's money. Clear lines of demarcation must be established.

    2. There must be an understanding that the tithes and offerings of the church do not belong to the pastor even if he is the unquestionable founder and leader of the church. Because of this, a pastor must not randomly access the church funds for personal needs.

    3. The pastor must not receive the church's tithes and offerings into his personal account.

       Offerings must not be kept in the pastor's home. It is wise for the pastor not to count money himself, but to delegate that task to a team of honest Christians.

4. A pastor should desist from taking money directly from the offering. Those who count money will consider you to be an unprincipled thief.

5. Do not borrow money from the church with the intention of paying back later.

6. Do not use your money for church projects with the intention of being paid back later.

Chapter 10

How to Manage Offerings

Prevent the loss of your offerings by the following measures:

i. Prevent stealing of the offerings by monitoring who becomes an usher.

ii. Keep the ushers in view at all times so that none of them is able to dip his fingers into the offering bags.

iii. Ensure adequate security so that an intruder cannot steal the offerings.

iv. Prevent the loss of offerings by ensuring that two or three people count the money at the same time.

v. Make sure that no one is ever left alone with the money. While they are alone, they can steal the money.

vi. You must have a form that indicates how much money was counted for the day. This form must be signed by at least two people. Whatever is on this form must correspond with the bank pay-in slips.

vii. Keep the money in a secure safe to ensure that the offering is not stolen after it has been counted.

viii. Offerings should not be kept in the pastor's house, as he will be accused of misusing the church's money.

ix. Bank the money at the very next opportunity. In between the time you receive the money and the time you do the banking, money can be misappropriated.

x. Ensure that 100% of your offerings are banked and banked promptly.

xi. Do not take out money from the offering before it is taken to the bank. This will confuse the accounts and open the door to all kinds of malpractices. If you need petty cash, sign a cheque of a fixed amount and enter this as your petty cash imprest.

Chapter 11

How to Improve Tithes and Offerings in the Church

1. Dedicate enough time during the service for receiving offerings.

2. From time to time, teach the church about giving. Regular and weekly teaching on giving tends to lose its impact. But irregular, spontaneous and Spirit-led teachings on giving, tend to boost offerings remarkably.

3. Show the congregation evidence of judicious use of money. Church members lose interest in giving, when they feel they are just financing the lifestyle of their superman pastor.

    I constantly mention the different projects, which we are engaged in so that my people are motivated.

4. Flow prophetically when receiving offerings. The people respond more to the power of God, than to human efforts to raise funds.

5. Take at least two offerings in each service. Initially, you would think that people would divide their offering into two. But experience has shown that taking two offerings approximately doubles the income realized from offerings. Also, there are many people who come to church late and they must also be given the opportunity to give their offerings.

6. Teach about tithing.

7. Link tithing with church membership. In other words let the people understand that you consider their tithe as the indication of their genuine membership.

8. Establish real differences between the tithe and every other offering. There must always be some indication that the

tithe is different from every other offering. For instance, the tithe could be paid through envelopes and cards whereas other offerings would not be.

9. Although opportunities for receiving the tithe should be made at every service, the first Sunday of a month should be set aside as a special Sunday for the receiving of tithes.

10. In line with the concept of distinguishing the tithe, church members can be made to come to the altar to present their tithe, whilst the offering basket could be passed round for all other offerings.

11. Create an index number system for the church. Encourage the members to write this number on the tithing card or envelope. Use a computer to monitor the tithes received. Many people would prefer to have a number on the envelope rather than their names. Not everyone would like people to know how much their tithe is.

12. Separate the record of the names and numbers of church members so that this information is kept private.

    This ensures some confidentiality for members who may not want just anybody to know how much contribution they make to the ministry.

13. Make the tithing records available so that church members can request a statement of their contributions.

14. When the need arises, use these records as a basis to determine who is a member and who is not.

    You can use these records to determine whom the church can assist.

Chapter 12

How to Raise Funds in the Church

1. Understand that fund-raising is intended to be a boost to the general tithes and offerings collected.

2. If you do not establish the basic income from tithes and offerings, fund-raising will never achieve its intended effect.

3. Special fund-raising events must not be too frequent in one congregation.

    Members quickly get tired of their pastor's fund-raising gimmicks and will no longer respond to appeals.

4. The fund-raiser must decide on the highest amount to be requested.

    When the amount is too high, he will get few responses. If no one responds to your initial high request, the entire fund-raising event could fall into jeopardy. I have seen this happen many times.

5. It is sometimes better to choose an average amount that many more people can respond to.

    For instance, in many congregations, there are more people who can give a hundred dollars and much fewer that can give a thousand dollars. Simple arithmetic shows us that sixty people giving one hundred dollars yields more than two people giving a thousand dollars each.

6. During fund-raising, give opportunities to all levels of givers to contribute, from the richest to the poorest.

    The poor people may collectively give more than the rich. You may therefore miss your target if you concentrate only on the rich.

7. Pledges are promises of money that Christians make during fund-raising events.

    Generally speaking, the shorter the time given for individuals to honour their pledges, the higher the returns will be. A few days after making pledges, many Christians forget the promises they made in church. I recommend that the period of time to pay up a pledge should be from one week to three months.

8. No matter how much people pledge, a wise pastor should not expect more than 30% of pledges to come in.

    Unfortunately, most Christians are not spiritual and do not keep their word. Many pledge large amounts and do not pay up. If you want to plan successfully you must never budget on what the congregation has pledged.

9. Pastors who budget on promised amounts are usually accused of misusing funds because the full amounts are never realized.

    It is wise to save money towards a project before embarking on fund-raising for it. This ensures that your project comes on whether the people pay up their pledges or not.

10. Never see fund-raising as a means of financing your projects.

    The build-up of your regular tithes and offerings should be the main source of project financing. In other words, see fund-raising as what it really is: a boost to your existing financial situation. God has determined how the church is to be financed: through regular tithes and offerings.

Section 5

CHURCH GROWTH AND THE MANAGEMENT OF CHURCH MEMBERS

Chapter 13

Define Who Your Members Are

Church members are the most valuable assets of a church. Your vision for church growth is realized as you have more and more church members. It is important to be able to count them and have accurate facts and figures at your fingertips.

Church members are difficult to count because they come and go so easily. Many of them do not tell you when they come; neither do they bother to tell you when they are leaving. Because of this, many churches do not have a true and accurate count of who really belongs to them.

Apart from this many pastors cannot tell where they stand in terms of their church growth vision. They cannot tell when the church is growing and whether they are accomplishing their vision for growth.

Many pastors cannot tell how many lawyers, doctors, fishermen or teachers there are in their churches. But this is important information because it will guide you in all your interaction with the congregation.

In this section allow God to birth in your spirit the importance of having accurate data and information. I pray that a data centre will be birthed in your ministry through this book. There is no need to give vague answers about the state of your church anymore. There is no need to tell lies about how many people come to our churches anymore. You can develop a powerful data centre for your mega church today!

1. **Register all your members using a simple membership registration form.**

   Having a complicated form with all sorts of details often creates useless data that is never used. The church is not the Central Intelligence Agency and does not require such extensive information.

2. **The most important fields of information for church membership are the names, ages, gender, telephone numbers and addresses.**

Some will argue that further information such as previous marriages; number of children, educational background, etc. are relevant for good pastoral care.

I agree with you, but my experience is that most of this information is never properly used or managed.

It becomes piles of useless data that no one knows what do with.

3. **Give every member a life-time index number which will be used as a permanent reference point.**

This number will be needed by every computer system and programme used. The index number will be used to monitor the individual's tithes. It can also be used by the individual in any activity that requires identification. For instance, if you have classes or examinations in the church, this number will come in handy.

4. **Do not be deceived! Many church members do not consider their membership as very important.**

When they are moving to another location or country, many church members do not bother to inform their pastor that they are leaving. They see themselves as insignificant members whose absence will not be noticed.

5. **The unannounced departure of numerous members without notice, converts your laboriously acquired information into useless data.**

This is why unnecessary and lengthy efforts to gather information about each member should be discouraged.

6. **Accept that church membership is fluid in its composition.**

There are always some stable and unmovable people in each congregation but it is best for every pastor to accept the absolute fluidity of church membership. Church membership can be described as a flowing river in which the water you see today will not be the water you see tomorrow.

7. **Make it easy to join the church.**

The filling of a simple form is an easy single procedure for joining the church. Some churches insist on people going through various classes and procedures before they are allowed to become members. This is a good idea but the danger is that many will not go through these classes and will assume that they are not members. I believe that as they join the church through a simple procedure, they will then have the opportunity to go through the classes.

8. **Accept the reality of different levels of member-ship.**

Within every congregation, there are at least four levels of membership:

i. Members who have filled a simple form.

ii. Members who are tithers.

Tithing indicates a level of commitment and Christian maturity.

iii. Members who participate in small groups and weekday (non Sunday) services.

Such people are even more committed.

iv. Members who are leaders.

There are people who in addition to all three descriptions above, become leaders and workers in the church. This fourth level is a crucial level because it is here that the moral and ethical standards of the church can be enforced. You cannot prevent homosexuals from filling forms. Neither can you prevent prostitutes from paying tithes or participating in church activities. You can only preach to them and pray that the Lord shows mercy. However, you can actually prevent a known or practising immoral person from occupying a position of leadership. This is the only way that the integrity of the church can be safeguarded–at the level of the leader's membership.

9. **Registering church members can provide important data which is useful in providing programmes and pastoral care to registered members.**

   Use computers, databases, and any other gadgets to manage the fluid membership of the modern church.

10. **Do not over-extend yourself in the field of computerization and administration.**

    There are many diversions and time-wasting traps which can cause a pastor to leave his true calling.

11. **Do not inflate figures of membership.**

    The greatest person in Heaven will not be the pastor with the most members; it will be the pastor who was most humble while on this earth.

Chapter 14

What to Expect from the Average Church Member

A successful mega church pastor is someone who understands the mindset of the average church member. Without a clear understanding of how church members think and operate, you will not succeed in administering the church.

The following points describe in a general way (of course, there are many exceptions) the mindset of the average church member. Financial planning by an administrator must take into account these realities. A successful pastor must predict certain trends and circumvent them.

The quicker you understand and predict these trends and circumvent them, the more successful you will be in ministry.

Pastors must not have an erroneous impression that their members really love God and that their minds are constantly on the church and its projects.

1. Most church members are not thinking about the church but about themselves.

2. They spend a lot of money on themselves, but very little money on God.

3. Most church members feel that a hundred dollars is little money in a shopping mall but is too much to give as offering in church.

4. Many church members do not pay tithes and they will not do so no matter what you say!

5. If you preach about tithes, some people will pay up for a while but most people will stop when they forget the message. Your financial planning as an administrator must take this into account.

6. Most church members will pledge various amounts of money during fund-raising events. However most of them will not pay what they promise. A wise pastor must expect only a small percentage of the pledged amount.

7. Most church members are irregular in their church attendance.

   These members therefore only contribute irregularly to the ministry. This accounts for the unpredictable and low income of churches. Any wise planner must take into account this unpredictable behaviour.

8. Most church members are ignorant of the sacrifices their pastor makes. Many church members think their pastor's only duty is to rest all week and deliver one Sunday sermon. This makes the average church member unwilling to make many financial sacrifices for the ministry.

9. Most people are inherently ungrateful. They benefit from the church but refuse to express their gratitude through contributions and gifts. The ingratitude of church members is demonstrated by the amounts of money people are willing to give to the ministry.

10. Many church members have commitments to other groups such as political parties, old boys' associations, tribal associations and professional bodies. Their commitment to these groups is often stronger than their commitment to the church. Know that many church members will readily sacrifice you and your church programmes for other engagements.

Section 6

CHURCH GROWTH AND THE HELPS MINISTRY

Chapter 15

How to Choose
Helps Ministers

Then the twelve called the multitude of the disciples unto them, and said, It is not reason that we should leave the word of God, and serve tables.

Wherefore, brethren, look ye out among you seven men of honest report, full of the Holy Ghost and wisdom, whom we may appoint over this business.

Acts 6:2-3

As a church grows, a new group of people will become important. These are the helps ministers! At the beginning of a church, a helps ministry does not seem very important. The pastor is the jack-of-all-trades and has to help himself accomplish whatever he needs to.

But with the growth of a mega church, you will need people to help in many areas. New problems will arise that will require the input of helps ministers. Helps ministers are there to solve problems in different areas of expertise.

A helps minister is someone who stays in the background but helps you to accomplish great things for the Lord. Such people are usually administrators, secretaries, personal assistants, special aides and special envoys. Although helps ministers are not publicly acknowledged, their role often converts a little known pastor into a fruitful and well-known minister.

Your willingness to accept that you need such helps ministers and your ability to successfully blend them into the ministry will determine how big your church can become.

I can remember how I declared that I did not and would not work with any women. Unfortunately for me, many of the helps ministers were women. I had to adapt to and accept their existence and presence in the ministry. My unwillingness to do so would have spelt failure in many areas of ministry.

Sadly, some people posing as helps ministers have destroyed entire ministries. Indeed, helps ministers can make or break an entire ministry.

Principles for Choosing Helps Ministers

1. Employ people that are genuinely needed by the organization.

2. Employ people from within the church. As much as possible, employ people who are church members. Sometimes it is not possible to do so. But it is better to take from amongst your own sheep.

3. Readily dismiss people from your organization. Anyone who employs people must be ready and willing to dismiss these people in the future if the need arises. Contrary to traditional opinion, it is important to fire non-performing staff members even though they may be members of your church.

4. Employ as few people as you possibly can.

   When people are employed for non-existent jobs, they become disgruntled and dissatisfied. Such people complain and create a discontented atmosphere in the church office. It is better not to have an employee than to have an unhappy employee.

5. Make employees carry out multiple roles. For instance, a pastor could be a lecturer at the Bible school and at the same time do pastoral duties. You may not need to have a secretary as many people can type their letters on their own. You may not need to have a receptionist as you could have a doorbell to announce the arrival of a visitor.

6 Wherever possible, use equipment instead of human beings.

   Machines do not get tired! Machines do not develop moods and attitudes! Machines do not ask to be paid for over-time work. Machines do not go on leave. Machines do not go on maternity leave. Machines do not resign suddenly!

7. Do not neglect professional and technical aspects of the ministry. You should have some knowledge about many professions. Many pastors have a "black-out mentality" and think they are not qualified to discuss certain things.

For instance, as soon as some ministers realize that something has to do with legal work they black-out and call for lawyers saying, "This is legal work, just call the lawyers to take over." In this way, pastors unsuspectingly sell their fate to misguided professionals who do not have their vision.

Whether it is accounting, medicine, law, architecture or engineering, there is a level to which you must be able to understand and discuss issues. You must read a lot and ask many questions. It takes humility to ask questions about things you do not know.

But by asking many questions, you will learn a lot about many things that you are clueless about. You can have sensible discussions with all the professional groups in your church. Bankers, travel agents, lawyers, accountants, human resource managers, carpenters, contractors, engineers, architects and administrators are supposed to be able to explain what they are doing in simple language. With the passage of time they will develop a healthy respect for your ability to engage in intelligent discussions on different subjects.

Chapter 16

Guidelines for Employing Helps Ministers

1. **Put everything in writing.** Once you begin to employ people, it is important to write letters and contracts where necessary. Discussions are not sufficient basis for dealing with employees even though they may be church members.

2. **Let education be the basis of employment.** Although the success of ministry is not dependent on education, it is an important factor. Education greatly refines the natural gifts that God has given to every individual. Any kind of education is often valuable even in the ministry.

    Your education does not have to be in a particular field in order to be valuable in that field. For instance, I am trained as a doctor but I function as a pastor, a manager, a doctor and a leader. I was not trained for much of what I do today but my general education in the fields of anatomy, physiology, pharmacology, microbiology etc. have greatly enhanced my managerial skills.

    Generally speaking, the more formally educated a person is, the more valuable he is. That is why salaries jump as individuals acquire more degrees.

    However, this is not a hard and fast rule. Some people are able to informally educate themselves thus making up for a lack of formal education. Another important effect of education is the establishing of discipline in the individual.

    The discipline that a person develops to go through exams is important. Generally speaking, an educated person is more disciplined than an uneducated person.

    The disciplines of education (having to stay up late, having to pass exams, having to overcome various barriers and hurdles) are all exercises that prepare the individual for the rigours of real life.

3. **Place people according to their temperaments.** Know all about temperaments. The knowledge of an individual's temperament is the best guide for placing him. Unfortunately, someone may be educated in an area but does not have the right temperament for that kind of work.

If you do not understand the strengths and weaknesses of the choleric, the melancholic, the phlegmatic and the sanguine you will be a frustrated employer. You will constantly wonder why the work is not done even though you have someone who is a specialist in that field.

Choose a choleric when you need a driving manager. The choleric is good at jobs that involve targets and deadlines. He is also good at pioneering new projects and doing things that have not been done before. He is also good at supervising others because of his natural tendency to take charge.

Because he is self-motivated and self-supervising, he is able to drive through the obstacles of a big project. A choleric person will spontaneously work for many extra hours. He or she can handle a number of different functions at the same time. The choleric is not usually good at being an assistant.

Choose a melancholic when the job involves being meticulous and detailed. A melancholic employee will also do well in positions where books and records must be kept. They are also target-oriented and very focused.

A melancholic may also be good for jobs that require secrecy. Melancholic people are very intelligent and very loyal.

Use them for sensitive jobs that require loyalty. Because they are very analytical and detailed they are also good at jobs that involve technical things. They are usually the best at using computers, machines and other technical equipment.

Choose the phlegmatic when there is a monotonous job. Repetitive work within already defined structures is the best place for the phlegmatic worker. Teaching in a school setting and doing routine work in an established office are good examples of jobs for the phlegmatic.

They are usually not good at meeting deadlines and building new projects. The phlegmatic is easy-going and may be the best person to handle difficult people situations. He may not always express the urgency required in sensitive situations and sees no need to hurry about anything. Keep your phlegmatic away from stressful and high intensity work zones.

The sanguine must be employed when the job requires intelligence, skill-giftedness, and the creation of happiness and pleasant conditions. The sanguine is good at jobs that have to do with human relationships. They usually give a good public presentation of your office and what you stand for.

They are often good singers because they are uninhibited and therefore give full expression to the music they perform. They introduce life and vitality to almost every circumstance. The sanguine is usually gifted and must be used in his gifted areas and not in the area of organization.

Somehow the sanguine is not very good at meticulous management and organization. Your sanguine employee may look outwardly charismatic, but is often not disciplined enough to carry things through.

4. **Supervise everything.** There are four main ways to supervise:

a. Supervision by meetings

Meetings provide a forum for discussion of the work. During these meetings, different aspects are discussed and the employees are made to focus on the important targets.

b. Supervision by visits

There are two types of visits: announced visits and unannounced visits. Announced visits help the individuals to put up their best performance. Surprise visits help the manager to see the real picture.

c. Supervision by monitoring targets

This is the best form of supervision. Ultimately, the worker is supposed to produce results. A result-oriented work place is often more fruitful than others.

d. Supervision by the "scapegoat" principle

In this method, workers who are found to be non-performing can be dismissed as an example to the others. In all my experience, there is nothing that sends a more sombre message than the dismissal of an employee. A tone of seriousness is introduced into the system by the dismissal of one person.

5. **Be a benevolent employer.** Be kind and generous to your staff. It is important for people to perceive that you genuinely care for them. Even if you do not have a good salary to offer, show them love.

   You will be surprised to find out that people will work for *"more love and less money", than for "more money and less love.*

Chapter 17

How to Employ a Helper

Step 1: The application letter

An application letter is to be written by the potential employee. This is important so that the individual will not say that he was forced to work in the ministry against his will. The application is the evidence of the individual's desire to work with you.

Step 2: Presentation of documents by the applicant

There should be a presentation of CVs and certificates from school. This is important because there are many who claim to have certain backgrounds but in actual fact have no real qualification. Some people attended university but either did not complete their courses or did not pass their exams.

Step 3: The temperament examination

A simple test can reveal the basic temperament of your potential employee. Ensure that you put your employee in an area that is suitable for his temperament.

Step 4: The general interview

Every applicant must be interviewed by a panel. A panel is better able to objectively assess an applicant. The interview helps create a solid foundation for the future. The panel becomes convinced about the rightness or wrongness of employing this individual. The job seeker defends his application and makes a case for his employment.

The interview helps the applicant to perceive the church as a professional, efficient and competent organization. This interview establishes whether the individual is the right person for the job or not.

Step 5: The financial interview

This interview centres on the financial package that the newly employed person can expect to receive. Sometimes it is wise to separate financial discussions from discussions centred on the job itself. In a church setting it is important that people work because they believe God has called them, rather than for the money. After this interview, if the individual is still happy to work for the organization then you may go ahead and give him the letter of appointment.

Step 6: The letter of appointment

A letter of acceptance of the applicant must be given to him when he passes the interview. This letter should specify the date of commencement of work. Such a letter would remove doubts concerning his date of employment. The date of employment becomes important when determining benefits that are time-related.

Step 7: The remuneration package letter

This is a letter that indicates the remuneration package that has been discussed at the financial interview. This includes things like the take home salary, and any other housing, transport or health benefits that may exist.

This includes what the person will be paid and what the person can expect in the future. It is wise to retain such letters.

Step 8: The job description letter

Give a letter containing the job title and the job description. This should explain in detail the job that the person is expected to do. Explain in your letter how the individual will be assessed and what targets should be accomplished. This letter should be delivered at an extensive and explanatory meeting.

Step 9: The orientation letter

This letter should introduce other existing departments and indicate the functions of other staff members. There will be many questions on the mind of a new person. For instance:

- Where should I go if I need money to complete a project?

- Who do I call on when I need equipment?

- Where do I go when I need equipment to be fixed?

- Where do I go when I personally need financial assistance?

- Who do I see when my computer breaks down?

- Who do I see when I need a car?

- Who do I see if I need to arrange for transport?

- What do I do if I want to resign?

- Who is my boss?

- Who does my boss report to?

Step 10: The general expectations letter

This is a letter that indicates the other general expectations of an employee as well as any staff rules that may exist. In some offices, there may be dress codes and rules about privacy and confidentiality. There may be rules about the use of equipment and the repair of equipment. There may also be rules about visitors to the office and access to the offices. There may be working hours that are peculiar to the office. All these and more need to be spelt out clearly.

Step 11: The sanctions letter

This is a letter that indicates a sanctions package. It should include measures that will be taken against an employee in the event of unsatisfactory performance or behaviour. Such sanctions must always include the possibility of dismissal. You must also include the reality of the need to lay off staff in the event that the church can no longer sustain its staff.

How to Determine Salaries

The employer must determine salaries. It is good to use a board to determine salaries. The board must have a formula that guides them in determining salaries.

It is important to establish clear grades and ranks among employees. These ranks must be understood and accepted by all. The basis for rank is the same basis for determining salaries. Ranks amongst the employees become the basis for different grades of benefits.

Salaries are always determined by the following principles:

a. The real cost of living

There is no point in paying someone less than he can survive on. You will only create an army of petty thieves within your offices. The cost of living varies from country to country. It even varies within a country. It is important to consider these realities. In some places people earn a lot of money but have equally high bills.

b. The salary which the individual was paid in his previous workplace

This serves as a good measure to what the person has lived on in the past. People often inflate their former salaries. Knowing the previous salary helps to silence individuals who may claim that you are not paying them well. All you have to do is to refer them to their previous jobs.

c. Comparable salaries

Salaries can be determined by knowing what is being paid to individuals who are doing similar jobs in comparable organizations. A secretary who demands an unreasonable salary must be told what other secretaries earn in comparable organizations. A pastor who demands outrageous benefits must be told about what other pastors earn in other churches.

d. The educational background of the individual

Generally speaking, the more educated a person is, the more he earns. There are times, however, that the qualifications of an individual must be ignored. There are some people who are good at passing exams in school and therefore have many degrees. Unfortunately, many of such people are of little practical use when it comes to real work. It must be remembered that a certificate is just a piece of paper and does not mean that an individual is capable of carrying out a job.

e. The value of the individual to the organization

This is the most important factor in determining someone's income. Consider what would happen if a particular employee were absent. Easily replaceable people, such as drivers and secretaries are not as valuable as managers and lifelong assistants!

f. The length of time the individual has worked after school

Usually, the longer an individual has been in gainful employment, the more mature and productive he is. Young people are full of zeal and energy but sometimes lack the maturity that seasoned workers have.

g. The length of time the individual has worked for the organization

The length of time that individuals have worked for you must be recognized. Generally speaking, the longer people work, the more they must be paid.

h. The ability of the organization to pay the individual

It is all well and good to propose very high salaries. Will the church be able to continue paying these salaries? Many organizations are unable to pay their employees at the end of the month. Over-staffing and over-paying people sometimes create this unfortunate situation. The leader must assess carefully whether he will be able to sustain certain levels of payment.

Sometimes, individuals want to be paid as though they work in a bank. I often tell my employees that we are neither a bank nor a gold mine. A secretary working for a gold mine may obviously have a higher salary than a secretary working for a church. A church simply does not have the income that a gold mine has and therefore cannot sustain the salaries that a gold mine pays.

Section 7

CHURCH GROWTH, CONVENTIONS AND CAMP MEETINGS

Chapter 18

How Camp Meetings Cause Church Growth

...and the number of the disciples MULTIPLIED...

Acts 6:7

A camp is a special time when a section of the church goes away to a secluded place to wait on God. During these days, there is usually intensified preaching, teaching and fellowship. These days of intense quality fellowship and spiritual impartation leave indelible imprints in the hearts of the participants.

There is something about a camp, which is different from a Sunday or weekday service. A camp has a powerful spiritual impact on all who attend. Camps cause great growth to come to the churches.

The Special Environment of a Camp

1. **A camp has a timeless environment.** The difference in the quality of fellowship is brought about by the timelessness of a camp. A camp is timeless because people do not have to rush home by any particular time. There is no closing time for the preaching and teaching. There is no need to cut down, cut back or cut off anything that is necessary for the people.

2. **A camp has a tension-free environment.** Tension is created by the presence of people who know it all. Proud people do not usually come for camps. They are usually too big to be found at such meetings. A camp automatically eliminates a group of stiff, fussy and difficult-to-please church members.

3. **A camp has an anxiety-free environment.** Anxiety is created by the cares of this world. The cares of this world are the legitimate needs, and concerns of the congregation.

At a camp, we are cut off from the outside world for a few days. The worries, cares and problems of the world are suspended for a while as we focus on the Lord.

4. **A camp has a patient environment.** Patience is important when training pastors. Jesus told His disciples to wait for Him and they did. They patiently sat under the trees and slept till Jesus reappeared.

Without patience, you will not see, hear nor feel many aspects of the glory of God.

5. **A camp has a humble environment.** The need to stay for long hours eliminates proud people from the congregation and leaves you with a group that are more teachable and open to receive.

Powerful Effects of Assembling for a Camp

1. **Camp meetings allow the Word to be spoken with boldness.** The absence of the proud know-it-all allows the Word of God to come forth freely.

And when they had prayed, the place was shaken where they were assembled together; and they were all filled with the Holy Ghost, and *they spake the word of God with boldness.*

Acts 4:31

2. **Camp meetings allow the Word of God to be preached extensively which causes a great increase in the number of disciples.**

And the word of God increased; and the number of the disciples multiplied in Jerusalem greatly; and a great company of the priests were obedient to the faith.

Acts 6:7

3. **Camp meetings allow important interaction between believers.**

And *all that believed were together*, and had all things common;

Acts 2:44

4. **Camp meetings allow many hours of prayer to take place.**

And when they heard that, *they lifted up their voice* to God with one accord, and said, Lord, thou art God, which hast made heaven, and earth, and the sea, and all that in them is:

Acts 4:24

5. **Camp meetings encourage oneness and unity so that the whole church has one heart and one soul.**

And *the multitude of them that believed were of one heart and of one soul*: neither said any of them that ought of the things which he possessed was his own; but they had all things common.

Acts 4:32

6. **Camp meetings give room for prophesies at church which charge up the people.**

He that speaketh in an unknown tongue edifieth himself; but *he that prophesieth edifieth the church.*

1 Corinthians 14:4

7. **Camp meetings give room for the manifestation of spiritual gifts which lead to the edifying of the church.**

Even so ye, forasmuch as ye are zealous of spiritual gifts, seek that ye may excel to the edifying of the church.

1 Corinthians 14:12

8. Camp meetings counteract the devil's work of division.

These are the ones who cause divisions, worldly-minded, devoid of the Spirit.

Jude 19 (NASU)

9. Camp meetings fight separation and isolation that comes from pride and sensuality.

These be they who separate themselves, sensual, having not the Spirit.

Jude 19

10. Camp meetings are gatherings which prevent the scattering of the sheep and deprive the devil of meat.

And they were scattered, because there is no shepherd: and they became meat to all the beasts of the field, when they were scattered.

Ezekiel 34:5

Chapter 19

How Conventions Cause Church Growth

... And the Lord ADDED to the church daily such as should be saved.

Acts 2:46-47

Conventions are simply gatherings of God's people. Conventions lift up the name of Jesus and always bring an air of celebration and victory. At these gatherings, many things take place which are spiritually positive and which lead to church growth. At conventions, the church usually enjoys the ministry of guest preachers. Convention speakers are often well received because they have the aura of a visitor.

Below is a list of powerful things that happen when gatherings of the saints occur. The gathering of the saints is what we call a convention. The more powerful conventions you have, the more your church will grow.

Powerful Effects of Gathering for Conventions

1. **Church conventions are important because the sheep are fed with good pasture.**

   I will feed them in a good pasture, and upon the high mountains of Israel shall their fold be: there shall they lie in a good fold, and in a fat pasture shall they feed upon the mountains of Israel.

   Ezekiel 34:14

2. **Church conventions are important because they allow healing power to flow.**

   And Jesus departed from thence, and came nigh unto the sea of Galilee; and went up into a mountain, and sat down there. And great multitudes came unto him, having with

them those that were lame, blind, dumb, maimed, and
many others, and cast them down at Jesus' feet; and he
healed them:

Matthew 15:29-30

3. Conventions of the saints are important because they bring the presence of God.

For where two or three are gathered together in my name,
there am I in the midst of them.

Matthew 18:20

4. Conventions of the saints are important because evil spirits are driven out of people.

And there was in their synagogue a man with an unclean
spirit; and he cried out

Mark 1:23

5. Conventions of the saints are important because they enable praise to go on.

And they, continuing daily with one accord in the temple,
and breaking bread from house to house, did eat their meat
with gladness and singleness of heart

PRAISING GOD, and having favour with all the people.
And the Lord added to the church daily such as should be
saved.

Acts 2:46-47

6. Conventions of the saints are important because they allow people to be saved.

And they, continuing daily with one accord in the temple,
and breaking bread from house to house, did eat their meat
with gladness and singleness of heart

Praising God, and having favour with all the people. And
THE LORD ADDED TO THE CHURCH DAILY such as
should be saved.

Acts 2:46-47

7. **Conventions of the saints are important because they allow the power of the Holy Ghost to shake the church.**

And when they had prayed, THE PLACE WAS SHAKEN where they were assembled together; and they were all filled with the Holy Ghost, and they spake the word of God with boldness.

Acts 4:31

In the name of our Lord Jesus Christ, when ye are gathered together, and my spirit, with the power of our Lord Jesus Christ1 Corinthians 5:4

8. **Conventions of the saints are important because they cause all needs to be met.**

Neither was there any among them that lacked: for as many as were possessors of lands or houses sold them, and brought the prices of the things that were sold

Acts 4:34

9. **Conventions of the saints are important because they enable spiritual gifts to operate. This causes the fear of God to be in the church.**

But a certain man named Ananias, with Sapphira his wife, sold a possession, And kept back part of the price, his wife also being privy to it, and brought a certain part, and laid it at the apostles' feet. But Peter said, Ananias, why hath Satan filled thine heart to lie to the Holy Ghost, and to keep back part of the price of the land? Whiles it remained, was it not thine own? and after it was sold, was it not in thine own power? why hast thou conceived this thing in thine heart? thou hast not lied unto men, but unto God. And Ananias hearing these words fell down, and gave up the ghost: and great fear came on all them that heard these things.

Acts 5:1-5

10. Conventions of the saints are important because they allow revelations, psalms and prophecies to come forth.

How is it then, brethren? when ye come together, every one of you hath a psalm, hath a doctrine, hath a tongue, hath a revelation, hath an interpretation. Let all things be done unto edifying.

1 Corinthians 14:26

Chapter 20

How to Have Successful Conventions

Three times a year you shall celebrate a feast to Me.
Exodus 23:14, NASB

1. Conventions should be held three times a year following the pattern of the feasts of Israel.

If you have more than three conventions, the events will lose their significance.

God ordained three main feasts for Israel. These feasts commemorated various significant events in the life of the nation Israel. They were to serve as reminders of significant things that the Lord taught them in their walk with Him.

There were seven different events that were grouped into three feast times. The Feast of Passover took place in the first month; the Feast of Pentecost took place in the third month, whilst the Feast of Tabernacles was held in the seventh month of the year.

2. Conventions are important events in the life of a church and people must take time off to attend and to participate.

On this same day you shall make a proclamation as well; you are to have a holy convocation. You shall do no laborious work. It is to be a perpetual statute in all your dwelling places throughout your generations
Leviticus 23:21, NASB

3. Everyone in the church must come for conventions. All males were to attend the festivals.

Three times a year all your males shall appear before the Lord GOD
Exodus 23:17, NASB

4. **Conventions must celebrate the salvation that the Lord has given us. Altar calls must be made during conventions. Sadly, Christian programmes are being held without altar calls for salvation.**

And ye shall observe the feast of unleavened bread; for in this selfsame day have I brought your armies out of the land of Egypt: therefore shall ye observe this day in your generations by an ordinance for ever.

Exodus 12:17

5. **Conventions must lead to much praise for God's goodness. There should be special times of praise and worship as well as special music.**

And the children of Israel that were present at Jerusalem kept the feast of unleavened bread days with great gladness: and the Levites and the priests praised the LORD day by day, singing with loud instruments unto the LORD.

2 Chronicles 30:21

6. **Conventions will raise funds for the house of the Lord. There must always be special times of fund-raising in the house of the Lord.** Conventions can greatly boost the finances of a church. Christians must be told to come to conventions expecting to give and to support the work of the Lord. They must not appear at a convention empty-handed.

Thou shalt keep the feast of unleavened bread: (thou shalt eat unleavened bread seven days, as I commanded thee, in the time appointed of the month Abib; for in it thou camest out from Egypt: and NONE SHALL APPEAR BEFORE ME EMPTY:)

Exodus 23:15

And thou shalt keep the feast of weeks unto the LORD thy God WITH A TRIBUTE OF A FREEWILL OFFERING of thine hand, which thou shalt give unto the LORD thy God, according as the LORD thy God hath blessed thee:

Deuteronomy 16:10

7. **Conventions bring about a feeling of joy, victory and celebration. These are important feelings that inspire church growth.**

And thou shalt rejoice before the LORD thy God, thou, and thy son, and thy daughter, and thy manservant, and thy maidservant, and the Levite that is within thy gates, and the stranger, and the fatherless, and the widow, that are among you, in the place which the LORD thy God hath chosen to place his name there.

Deuteronomy 16: 11

Section 8

CHURCH GROWTH AND RELATIONSHIPS

Chapter 21

Why Relationships and Friendships Lead to Church Growth

Iron sharpeneth iron; so a man sharpeneth the countenance of his friend.

Proverbs 27:17

Churches that do not grow are often isolated. Ministers of the Gospel who have good relationships with other ministers often become successful and take on the characteristics of their friends. It is important to have good friends in the ministry. You become like your friends. If your friends have large and successful churches you are likely to have a large and successful church too.

Silently living in isolation will not help anybody. It will definitely not help someone who wants his church to grow. Humble yourself and do what it takes to have relationships with those who matter.

Years ago, I zeroed in on Dr. Yonggi Cho and decided to learn from him and get close to him. Perhaps, that was one of the most important decisions of my life as a pastor. I had decided to become close to the pastor of the largest church in the world. That association has affected me in more ways than I can think.

Golf and Lunch

One day, after playing golf and fellowshipping privately with Dr Cho, I sat down to have lunch with him and some other ministers.

An elderly Korean gentleman walked up to me and said, "You have done very well. I remember you. I remember when you first came to meet with Dr Cho in Yverdon, Switzerland. You were unable to meet him, even though you wanted to."

That was almost twenty years ago.

Then he continued, "You have persisted. Do you remember me? I spoke to you then."

I smiled back at him, "I remember you clearly. I remember it like yesterday. I had just started my church and I did not even have a church building."

Then he said again, "You have really persisted."

You see, it had been a long and dogged journey of coming close to a great person. I had come from the outside, from nowhere. And here I was, sitting next to the pastor of the largest church in the world having lunch.

After years of associating I had become a golfer and also received the great spiritual blessing of becoming the pastor of a large church.

1. **You must have friendships, associations, relationships, affiliations and connections with other ministers of God.** Every minister and every relationship is a joint that supplies something to your life and ministry. What they supply to you will cause growth to happen in your ministry. Relationships with key ministers of God have greatly contributed to the growth of my ministry.

Relationships cause growth!

Interactions cause growth!

Friendships cause growth!

That is what the Bible says.

New dimensions and new chapters have opened up in my ministry as I have opened up to different people. Read it for yourself: ... the whole body, being fitted and held together by that which EVERY JOINT SUPPLIES, according to the proper working of each individual part, CAUSES THE GROWTH of the body for the building up of itself in love". (Ephesians 4:15-16 (NASB)

2. **You must have friends and relationships in the ministry because these relationships will give you KNOWLEDGE you do not have**. You are always excluded from certain things because of knowledge you do not have. In the ministry, it is necessary to relate with other ministers who may not be in your church or denomination. God wants to expose you to other ministry gifts.

...being darkened in their understanding, EXCLUDED FROM THE LIFE OF GOD, BECAUSE OF THE IGNORANCE that is in them, because of the hardness of their heart;

Ephesians 4:18 (NASB)

3. **You must have friendships and relationships because they stir you up for greater works in the Lord.** When you stay in your little world you have no idea of what God is doing elsewhere. You have no idea that there can be something greater and better than what you are doing. Every time I have visited someone's church I have been blessed and provoked to do something greater and better in my church.

And let us consider one another to PROVOKE UNTO love and to GOOD WORKS:

Hebrews 10:24

4. **You must have friends who will tell you the truth in love.** When the truth is spoken to you in love, it causes you to grow up. Is it not growth you are seeking? Is that not why you are reading this book? Hearing the truth causes you to grow up. That is what the Bible says.

Relationships with external ministers can expose you to the truth that you need to hear. You may not hear that truth in your own world because there may be no one with enough authority or exposure to tell you what you need to hear.

But speaking the truth in love, MAY GROW UP into him in all things, which is the head, even Christ:

Ephesians 4:15

5. **You must have associations in the ministry. Many blessings come by being associated with other blessed people.** My association with great men of God has been a tremendous source of blessing to me. One day, I was invited to a foreign country to preach. I wondered why the pastor had invited me. When I asked him why he had invited me, he said, "I saw you on a video with David Yonggi Cho. It seemed you were interpreting or doing something on the stage."

He said to me, "I invited you because anyone who is associated with David Yongi Cho must be a good person."

"Wow", I said to myself, "this is the clearest example of how you can be blessed just by being associated with someone else."

Laban, the non-believer, knew this principle very well. He told Jacob, God blessed me because you were in my camp. He recognized how, where and why blessings were coming to him.

And Laban said unto him, I pray thee, if I have found favour in thine eyes, tarry: for I have learned by experience that the Lord hath BLESSED ME FOR THY SAKE.

Genesis 30:27

6. **You must have friendships, associations, relationships, affiliations and connections with other ministers of God to avoid isolation.**

And the eye cannot say unto the hand, I have no need of thee...

1 Corinthians 12:21

Often, isolation occurs because one has been hurt in the early stages of ministry. Many ministers run into a corner to escape being despised.

Isolation can work together for your good.

Isolation helps you to concentrate on your ministry.

Isolation helps you avoid being despised, disregarded and discouraged all the time by other so-called successful ministers.

Isolation helps you to avoid the distractions of inter-church politics.

Isolation helps you to avoid the wholesale adoption of other ministers' mistakes.

Isolation helps you to develop your unique identity and calling.

Isolation helps you to avoid being submerged under the banners of other domineering pastors who are trying to assume lordship over all churches in the city.

Isolation will force you to learn biblical rather than human standards for all aspects of life and ministry.

But isolation can also work against you in the ministry because you will need the input, ideas and gifts of other ministers.

You may be able to learn a great deal from other successful pastors in your city. I have learnt a lot from those directly ahead of me in my city. I have watched and learnt from their mistakes and successes. I do things in my church that I have learnt from other ministers.

Chapter 22

How to Develop Important Ministerial Relationships

The key to developing ministerial relationships with other pastors is to invite them in an honourable way, treat them well and give them a memorable time in your company. This is the seed that can develop into lifelong relationships.

Most of the important relationships I have in the ministry have developed after I invited them to visit my church. Most of these friendships have grown over the years and become vital relationships for my ministry.

It starts with the invitation to the pulpit and develops into other areas although not all invitations have led to relationships.

Do not be surprised if some visiting ministers shun your friendship. Some people are not very relational and others may not be interested in a relationship with you.

Sometimes, people do not relate with you because they are intimidated by you. They may be afraid of you and will show it by rejecting you.

How to Develop Relationships through Invitations

1.   Treat your visiting minister as a very important person.

Everyone loves to be pampered and treated specially. The wrong handling of a visiting minister often leads to offences and the destruction of already fragile acquaintances.

Give your guest the best possible place to stay. Don't put him in a room with your children. Don't make him share a room with your children. You may not be able to afford the nicest hotel, but you must do what you can afford. Ministers tend to ask where other visiting preachers were hosted.

The Four-Room Hotel

One day, I was invited to a country to preach. I had travelled very far and spent many hours getting there.

When we arrived, we were taken to the dirtiest part of the city. The roads were literally strewn with rubbish. You could not take two steps without stepping into something. There was a big house right on the corner of this filthy area.

When we entered the house I asked, "Where is this?"

I was told that it was a hotel. I was surprised that they were calling it a hotel because it had only four rooms which opened into a common space. Also a family lived upstairs, above the four rooms. Apparently, the pastor saved a lot of money by using this building because his family owned it.

In the morning, a man would come up with a big plate of bread rolls in one hand and margarine in the other hand.

I asked, "What is this?"

He said, "This is for your breakfast."

I have never stayed in a dirtier place than that building. I was afraid to have my bath because I was afraid of the electric wires that were sticking out into the shower. I was afraid of turning in the bed because I did not want to touch more of the bed sheet with my body.

I settled into this four-room hotel and stayed there for a whole week.

I was happy to be there because I thought they were very poor and this was what they could afford.

Later in the week, I got to find out that this same ministry had hosted another man of God. "Wow", I thought to myself, "Did this man of God stay in this hotel?" I did some investigations and found out that he had actually been brought to this same four-room hotel.

As soon as he entered our four-room hotel he struck the table and said, "I am not staying here. Take me to the best hotel in this city!"

The host pastor scrambled to get the man of God a proper hotel.

"Are there other hotels in this town?" I asked.

"O yes, there are other nice places."

Later that week we passed by the hotel where this other man of God had been taken.

You see, people find out how you treated others. They compare. Ministers are very sensitive, always looking out to see if they are despised or respected.

2. Show honour to your friend by giving him an honourable invitation.

Do not invite someone you want to honour to a minor function. Invite the person to an important service that will be well attended. Invite people personally if you can and follow it up with a letter.

You must be present at the service for which you invited the person. Do not invite a minister if you know you will be absent (especially when building a new relationship).

The Man in Shorts

One day, I was invited by a man of God to minister in his church. I arrived in the city after a very long journey and it was already time to preach. My host, however, was at home wearing sports shorts and playing table tennis.

He asked that we be taken to the church where I was to speak. I found out that it was a minor programme that my host himself would not bother to attend.

I did not know the young man who introduced me to preach. He did not know me either and I did not know what role he played in the church.

As I preached, I wondered why I had come all this way to a programme that my host would not even attend himself.

3. The visiting minister should be welcomed at his point of entry.

If the external minister is coming from another location, as much as possible a minister of his rank must receive him at the airport, station, etc! For example, if he is a head pastor, then the senior minister of the inviting church must meet him and see him off.

In some cases it is not possible for the senior pastor to meet arriving guests at the airport or station. So an appropriate person must do that on his behalf.

4. Welcome your guest when he arrives in the church. Talk to him.

Sit next to him and relate with him!

Make friends with your guest and have good fellowship with him. It could be the beginning of a lifelong relationship. Don't spend all the time making excuses about the size of your church and the poor attendance of the convention. Every genuine pastor will appreciate the effort you are making to build the church.

5. Invite someone that you genuinely admire and respect.

Remember that secret criticism kills relationships. Do not criticize or ridicule your guest ministers. Why do you invite someone to your church only to criticize him behind his back? Do not speak evil of any minister or church, especially from the pulpit or in public. Do not entertain negative comments about guest ministers and their preaching whilst they are with you and when they are gone. I have had ministers of the Gospel who invited me and allowed their associates to criticize me after I left. If you have anything to say about a minister, say something positive.

... speak evil of no man...

Titus 3:2

Remember that the way you speak will set the stage for others to criticize you in the future.

The Windowless Room

You must show your guests that you respect them. Once I was invited to minister in a large church. I enjoyed ministering there but I had one problem. I was put in a guest house with a windowless room. The room I was living in didn't have "windows". There were windows but they were permanently closed and permanently covered with curtains. There was also no functioning air conditioner in the room.

This meant that this room was virtually windowless and airless. In the evenings, after ministering, I would go out and sit on the field to breathe in some fresh air. When I was sure that I had enough oxygen for the night, I would retire to my windowless room.

On one of the days, I found out that a great American preacher had also been invited to this church. So I asked, "Where did this American preacher stay when he came to minister here? Did he stay in this same windowless guest house?"

As I expected, the American minister was not put in my windowless room. He had been taken to a grand hotel and treated royally. Naturally, I felt that these people did not appreciate the gift of God and did not care for me as much as they did for their American guest.

Indeed, you must be careful how you treat ministers because they are always asking questions to find out if they are really respected, appreciated or even wanted.

6. **Refer to your invited guest by the official designation he has accorded himself.**

People have reasons for calling themselves Bishops, Reverends or Apostles. Ministers are sensitive about their titles. If his title is General Overseer, do not refer to him as the General Superintendent. If he refers to himself as an Apostle, do not call him a Pastor.

7. **Find out the full name of your guest and pronounce it properly.**

You must know the full name of your invited guest. There is nothing more disrespectful than a person who cannot bother to pronounce your name. Many African Americans had their names changed because their white slave masters could not bother to pronounce their African names. Do not refer to him as Reverend Ag when his name is Reverend Agegebodavari.

8. **Identify and introduce the visiting minister's delegation.**

It is important to acknowledge them as well. Do not disregard people's associates. You may be disregarding a future Elisha. The visiting minister's wife should also be welcomed nicely. She is an important person.

9. **Know the name of the invited minister's church or ministry.**

Not remembering the correct name of somebody's church makes you look arrogant. Don't give the impression that you are dealing with an unimportant church with an unfortunately laborious name. Don't give the impression that you cannot be bothered to remember the name of his ministry.

For instance, do not say he is the Pastor of The Light Church when he is the Pastor of Lighthouse Chapel International. There is a big difference between the two!

10. **Give your visiting minister enough time to minister.**

For example, do not give a guest minister 10 minutes to minister, when he has travelled long distances to be with you.

The Hand of God

One day I travelled to a far away land to minister. I had been invited by this man of God to be a speaker at a convention. The service was to close at about 8.00pm and I was supposed to start preaching at about seven o'clock.

To my surprise, instead of my host introducing me and handing over the microphone to me he began a teaching on "the hand of God". Indeed, it was a night of revelation as he taught on what the hand of God was.

He gave several examples of the hand of God at work in the Old Testament. Then he gave examples of the hand of God in the New Testament. Then he explained how the hand of God could change your life.

Then he taught on where the hand of God can be found today!

I sat for almost an hour as I listened to this wonderful message. But I couldn't help wondering why I had come all the way from Ghana. This man knew exactly what he wanted to minister to his people and to say the least, I felt silly sitting there.

Then, at the end of his message, I thought he would hand over to me so that I would preach the second message of the day. But it was not yet my turn because he announced that the hand of God had begun to move right there in the congregation.

Suddenly, the hand of God began to move in the congregation and people began to scream and fall down under the power. He ministered powerfully to the people for another twenty minutes.

By the time he finished, there was hardly anyone standing in the congregation. It was indeed a night of power and of the hand of God.

Finally, when it was past closing time, he announced that I had come from Ghana to also minister (there were people strewn all over the front of the church). What was I expected to do now?

I was indeed surprised that I was being called to speak after the service had clearly ended with the power of God evident and people lying all over the front.

Everyone in my entourage was bewildered. I have never forgotten this strange behaviour of my host. Obviously he did not really want me to come.

11. **Introduce your guest minister with excitement. Let the church welcome the visitor with great respect and expectation in their hearts.**

12. **Outline and explain specifically to your guest minister any function or expectation you may have of him.**

    For example, if you want him to raise funds, make altar calls, ordain pastors, etc., discuss this with him in detail before he arrives. Do not surprise your guest with unusual ceremonies with which he may not be comfortable. Don't put him on the spot and make him feel silly or inadequate.

13. **After preaching and ministering, the visiting minister should be refreshed briefly and then politely escorted away.**

14. **Ensure that your visiting minister will have good food that he can eat during his stay with you.**

Flamingo Stew

One day, I was invited to minister in a large church. We were put in a hotel which had very little ventilation. When it was supper time, the hotel was unable to provide food so the host sent some people to bring food to us.

As we sat around the dinner table, we were served with "chicken". But I was not sure whether it was a chicken because the legs of the chicken were so long and I had never seen such a long chicken leg before.

Honestly, I was not sure which bird I had been given. Perhaps it was a flamingo, perhaps it was an eagle, perhaps it was just a local bird. This was not the first time I had been given a local bird to eat. On another ministry trip I had been given a bird which had a completely different colour from what I was used to. Yet on another occasion I was served with a whole bird so small that it could fit into my palm.

Again and again people choose to give you the most easily caught bird in the area. Everybody calls the birds in their area "chicken". But experience will teach you that not all birds are chickens.

Try to give your guests food that they can eat and "chicken" that they will enjoy.

15. The conditions of your guest minister's visit should be clearly defined prior to his arrival and acceptance to minister.

Even so hath the Lord ordained that they which preach the gospel should live of the gospel.
1 Corinthians 9:14

The honorarium and all expenses can be discussed in many cases before the minister accepts the invitation. This includes financial, transportation, and accommodation arrangements. The minister must be given the option to decide whether he will come in spite of the conditions that you are offering him.

This is especially important if the minister is travelling a long distance. You may wrongly assume that the visiting minister will only incur the cost of his plane ticket.

But you may not know that he had to, for example, travel in a rented car 300km to the airport and sleep in a hotel overnight in order to be able to catch the plane in the morning. All of these are hidden expenses, which must be discussed. It is very sad for a minister to travel several miles, minister from his heart, only to return impoverished and in debt.

The Phone Call Invitation

One day, I received a phone call from a man of God inviting me to his church. He said he would be so honoured if I would come to minister in his church.

Then he asked, "Are there any conditions for your coming?"

I answered, "If you can pay for my ticket and where I would stay that should be fine."

He was happy and promised to do that. I travelled on several different flights and eventually landed in this country.

The first surprise was that we were taken to a hotel different from where he had told us we would be lodging. I quickly checked my secretary's notes and asked why we were being taken to a very different place. They mumbled an apology and took us to where they had earlier promised. I enjoyed my visit there and ministered powerfully.

Finally, when I was leaving, I was expecting to receive the money for my ticket. No such luck!

He did not pay for my ticket!

He did not give me any honorarium! What had happened? I had undertaken this journey entirely at my own expense, without planning to.

If you do this to visiting ministers, you will soon have a bad reputation and no one will come to you any more.

Seven Steps to a Good Honorarium

And as ye would that men should do to you, do ye also to them likewise.

Luke 6:31

1. A good honorarium should cover all the expenses of the visiting minister.

The honorarium must also bless and encourage the minister financially. A good honorarium must be judged by what you would like to receive if you were the guest.

2. A visiting minister's rank also determines what a good honorarium is.

    If the person is a very senior minister, the honorarium must be correspondingly substantial.

3. A good honorarium is calculated by the number of days a person ministers.

4. A good honorarium is also determined by the impact of the visiting minister's ministry.

5. Honorariums should not be given to the visiting minister in full public view. Do not let the visiting minister feel uncomfortable as he receives your envelope in the full view of everyone. Your guest should be given his honorarium in private and by the appropriate person.

6. The visiting minister may sign a voucher or receipt for the honorarium (for accounting purposes).

7. The honorarium should be prepared with an accompanying letter before the meeting.

    This is to avoid very long delays in paying the honorarium. Some churches even forget to pay any honorarium at all. It is often more difficult to pay the honorarium long after the minister has left than it is to pay immediately after the programme.

Section 9

CHURCH GROWTH AND GETHSEMANE

Chapter 23

How Church Growth Is Affected by Gethsemane

And He came out and proceeded as was HIS CUSTOM to the Mount of Olives; and the DISCIPLES ALSO FOLLOWED Him.

And when He arrived at the place, He said to them, "Pray that you may not enter into temptation."

And HE WITHDREW from them about a stone's throw, and He knelt down and began to pray,

saying, "Father, if Thou art willing, remove this cup from Me; YET NOT MY WILL, BUT THINE BE DONE."

Now an angel from heaven appeared to Him, STRENGTHENING HIM.

And being in agony He was praying very fervently; and His sweat became like drops of blood, falling down upon the ground.

And when He rose from prayer, He came to the disciples and found them sleeping from sorrow,

and said to them, "Why are you sleeping? Rise and pray that you may not enter into temptation."

Luke 22:39-46 (NASB)

The Principles of Gethsemane

1. **Gethsemane teaches us that the turning points for your life and ministry are determined in the private and personal times you have with the Lord.**

The turning point for Jesus' ministry came in the Garden of Gethsemane. Gethsemane was the place where Jesus received strength to accomplish the will of God. The turning point for your church will come when you wait on the Lord.

The turning point that will give you church growth will take place in your Garden of Gethsemane.

2. **Gethsemane shows us the greatest example of waiting on the Lord.** There is no man that is used of the Lord who has not interacted with the Lord deeply and personally.

   Moses encountered the Lord by the burning bush. It was that personal private burning bush meeting that propelled him into his worldwide ministry. It will be your personal private burning bush experience that will propel you into the church growth you desire.

   Jacob's meeting with the Lord also gave birth to his ministry of producing God's nation Israel.

3. **Gethsemane teaches us that you must have a place you go to often to wait on the Lord.** It must be part of your life's routine to visit Gethsemane regularly. According to the Scripture it was His custom to visit that garden in the Mount of Olives.

   And He came out and proceeded as was HIS CUSTOM to the Mount of Olives; and the disciples also followed Him.
   Luke 22:39, NASB

4. **Gethsemane teaches us the importance of going away from your usual environment and to places where you benefit from nature.** Nature tends to relax you and God's voice will reach you better when your mind and heart are relaxed. Nature itself has many messages contained within it.

5. **Gethsemane teaches us the importance of fellowshipping with your most senior friends and associates.** Gethsemane is a place where you can have important life-changing discussions with the most important people in your ministry.

6. **Gethsemane teaches us the importance of being alone with God.** Gethsemane is a place where you can receive life-changing revelations from the Lord. The disciples

received life-changing teachings about prayer. Without revelation you will not be different from the people you lead.

7. **Gethsemane teaches us the importance of praying, "Thy Will be done" for several hours.** Some people do not believe in repeating prayers. But if we are to follow the example of Jesus, we will spend hours praying. We will pray, "Thy will be done" for hours and hours on end.

Chapter 24

The Art of Waiting on God

Who hath woe? Who hath sorrow? Who hath contentions? Who hath babbling? Who hath wounds without cause? Who hath redness of eyes?

THEY THAT TARRY LONG at the wine ...

Proverbs 23:29-30

Wine changes those who tarry long at it. We are also affected as we stay longer and longer in His presence. The longer you tarry at the wine, the more you experience stronger effects of the wine. When you tarry long at the wine, you begin to babble uncontrollably and act strangely.

As you stay longer at the wine, your eyes turn red and you start to see things differently. Gethsemane teaches us that the longer we stay in the presence of God the more we get soaked and affected by Him.

Just as people learn to stay longer and longer at the wine bar, you must learn to stay longer in His presence. The longer you stay in His presence, the more you will experience the effect of God's presence.

1. *Develop the art of waiting on God all alone.*

And it came to pass in those days, that HE WENT OUT INTO A MOUNTAIN to pray, and continued all night in prayer to God.

Luke 6:12

Jesus went into the mountain to pray. After this prayer time he chose his disciples. There are times you must pray with others but there are times you must wait on the Lord alone. If you cannot spend long times praying on your own there is something wrong with you.

Remember that a minister is an ambassador of the Lord. You are a representative of Jesus Christ who is supposed to tell others about God. If you have never spent time with Him, what will you know and what will you share?

The Apostle John described his ministry as sharing and preaching what he had seen, known, handled and touched. "That which was from the beginning, which we have heard, which we have seen with our eyes, which we have looked upon, and our hands have handled, of the Word of life; ... That which we have seen and heard declare we unto you, that ye also may have fellowship with us: and truly our fellowship is with the Father, and with his Son Jesus Christ." (1 John 1:1-3).

2. Develop the art of waiting wait on God with a group of fellow ministers.

Let the priests, the ministers of the LORD, weep between the porch and the altar ...

Joel 2:17

Jesus is always present in a special way when we come together to wait on Him. The New Testament shows us how prophets and teachers ministered to the Lord and fasted. The Lord will speak when His ministers come together to wait on Him. "Now there were in the church that was at Antioch certain prophets and teachers; as Barnabas, and Simeon that was called Niger, and Lucius of Cyrene, and Manaen, which had been brought up with Herod the tetrarch, and Saul.

As they ministered to the Lord, and fasted, the Holy Ghost said, Separate me Barnabas and Saul for the work whereunto I have called them" (Acts 13:1-2).

3. Develop the art of waiting on God with the congregation.

Blow the trumpet in Zion, sanctify a fast, call a solemn assembly:

Gather the people, sanctify the congregation, assemble the elders, gather the children, and those that suck the breasts: let the bridegroom go forth of his chamber, and the bride out of her closet.

Joel 2:15-16

All through the Bible, the prophets called the people to come together to wait for His deliverance. This is an important pattern we must follow. If you want church growth you must develop the practice of calling the church together for fasting and long hours of prayer.

4. *Develop the art of waiting on God by timing yourself.*

... saith unto Peter, What, could ye not watch with me one hour?"

Matthew 26:40

Note the time at the start of your prayer session. Decide how long you are going to pray before you start. When you do that, you will be compelled to spend a decent period of time in prayer. Jesus was not impressed when Peter could not pray for one hour. He is the same yesterday, today and forever. He is equally unimpressed that you cannot pray for one hour.

If you do not note the time, you will think that you prayed longer than you actually did. You will tell yourself, "Oh, I must have prayed for two hours" when you only prayed for ten minutes.

Unless you are experienced in prayer, you will make wrong judgments about the length of time you have prayed. Nowadays, I can tell when I have prayed for an hour. Initially, I would pray for ten minutes and think it was an hour. This is why you need a clock when you are going to wait on the Lord.

5. *Develop the art of waiting on God in a church atmosphere.*

...Now bring me a minstrel. And it came to pass, when the minstrel played, that THE HAND OF THE LORD CAME upon him.

2 Kings 3:15

124

A church atmosphere is created by the sound of preaching and worship music. Playing DVDs of church services also create a church atmosphere.

Pray with some kind of preaching or music in the background. *The speed of preaching/music is a hundred times faster than the speed of silence.* This means that time runs a hundred times faster when there is some kind of background preaching or music.

Have you been there when people were asked to observe a minute's silence? Have you noticed how long the period of silence was? Did you know that they never really spend a whole minute of silence? A minute of silence is so long and so uncomfortable that people rarely spend a whole minute in silence.

This is because of the principle I just shared with you: *the speed of preaching/music is a hundred times faster than the speed of silence.*

When you pray with the sound of preaching or music in the background, time runs much faster! Before you know it, you would have spent several hours in prayer with the Lord!

The sound of the preaching of the Word of God creates the best atmosphere for spiritual things. Dear friend, we are constantly bombarded with the godless atmosphere of secular television and radio. That kind of atmosphere actually prevents prayer.

You need something that will keep you in a prayerful mood for at least one hour. Godly music creates a beautiful worship environment. I always play music or preaching in the background when I am praying.

Dear friend, the very atmosphere of our world is charged with demonic entities. The prince of the power of the air pollutes the very air we breathe. It is difficult to pray in such an environment. This is the reason why many Christians do not pray for long hours. They are trying to pray in a hard and difficult atmosphere.

But there is good news: You can have your own little church service wherever you are! The Spirit of the Lord can move over you in your car. Invest in whatever it takes to create the right prayer atmosphere.

The Spirit of the Lord will come upon you as you stay in the environment of anointed minstrels and preachers.

6.   *Develop the art of waiting on God by praying in tongues whilst you read the Bible and other ministry books.*

For if I pray in an unknown tongue, my spirit prayeth, but my understanding is unfruitful.

1 Corinthians 14:14

Because I pray in tongues for long periods, my mind is unfruitful and free for reading. I constantly read whilst I spend hours in prayer. My spirit prays to the Lord while my mind concentrates on the Bible that I am reading. This helps me to pray for even longer hours.

As you pray in tongues for hours, your spirit man will be edified and charged up.

7.   *Develop the art of waiting on God by praying with targets.*

And it came to pass in those days, that he went out into a mountain to pray, and continued ALL NIGHT IN PRAYER to God.

Luke 6:12

Set yourself targets for praying. You can set yourself a target of prayer by giving yourself a number of hours to pray. For instance, you can decide to pray for ten hours, twenty hours, forty hours or fifty hours. With a target of fifty hours, you are likely to need about six days to pray. Sometimes, setting the target in terms of hours is better than setting the number of days you want to wait on the Lord.

I have always felt that unless I spent a long time in prayer, I would not accomplish much. All the prayers I learnt from Jesus were prayers of many hours.

Jesus spent forty days in the wilderness.

Jesus prayed all night in the mountain before He chose His disciples.

Jesus prayed for a great while before day.

Jesus prayed for three hours in the Garden of Gethsemane.

These examples must be a guide for your prayer life. They will make you spend many hours of your life in prayer.

If you believe in these examples from the life and ministry of Jesus you will never be satisfied with five and ten minute prayers. You will desire to pray for lengthy periods of time.

8. Develop the art of waiting on God by praying with absolute fasting.

Absolute fasting is when you do not eat anything at all. Absolute fasting is an important exercise that makes you more spiritual and causes you to focus on God. For those who eat a lot and spend a lot of time eating, fasting provides a necessary break from a strong carnal distraction.

9. Develop the art of waiting on God by praying and fasting with "no pleasant bread" (instead of not praying and not eating at all).

In those days I Daniel was mourning THREE FULL WEEKS. I ate NO PLEASANT BREAD, neither came flesh nor wine in my mouth, neither did I anoint myself at all, till three whole weeks were fulfilled.

Daniel 10:2-3

Daniel fasted for twenty-one days. Daniel's fast involved eating, but eating what he described as "no pleasant bread". In other words, he stayed away from what he would really have loved to eat.

Staying away from your usual meals and your usual delights is a form of fasting. It is called "no pleasant bread" fasting.

It is better to have prayer and eat a bit than to do absolute fasting without praying.

Many people do absolute fasting without praying. Many times, absolute fasting actually prevents people from praying. At the end of their fasting time, many Christians have hardly spoken to the Lord. They use all their energy to survive the absolute fast and make it to 6.00pm when they can eat.

Why do I say it is better to pray and eat than to fast absolutely and not pray? Because all the promises Jesus gave to us had to do with prayer and not fasting. Jesus Christ promised to answer prayers. Jesus never promised to answer fasting. Understand what I am saying! Fasting is important for every Christian. Don't use this as a reason not to fast.

Look at the Word of God. Are the promises of reward for our prayers or for our fastings?

Look at just seven of the promises Jesus gave to people who would pray. These promises are the words of Jesus Christ Himself. Did He promise to answer fasting or did He promise to answer prayers?

Indeed, if I have to choose between fasting and praying I would choose to pray because Jesus has promised to answer prayers!

1. And whatsoever ye shall ask in my name, that will I do, that the Father may be glorified in the Son. If ye shall ask any thing in my name, I will do *it*.

    John 14:13-14

2. Ye have not chosen me, but I have chosen you, and ordained you, that ye should go and bring forth fruit, and that your fruit should remain: that whatsoever ye shall ask of the Father in my name, he may give it you.

    John 15:16

3. If ye abide in me, and my words abide in you, ye shall ask what ye will, and it shall be done unto you.

    John 15:7

4. And in that day ye shall ask me nothing. Verily, verily, I say unto you, Whatsoever ye shall ask the Father in my name, he will give it you.

    Hitherto have ye asked nothing in my name: ask, and ye shall receive, that "your joy may be full.

    John 16:23-24

5. Therefore I say unto you, What things soever ye desire, when ye pray, believe that ye receive them, and ye shall have them.

    Mark 11:24

6. And I say unto you, Ask, and it shall be given you; seek, and ye shall find; knock, and it shall be opened unto you.

    For every one that asketh receiveth; and he that seeketh findeth; and to him that knocketh it shall be opened.

    Luke 11:9-10

7. But thou, when thou prayest, enter into thy closet, and when thou hast shut thy door, pray to thy Father which is in secret; and thy Father which seeth in secret shall reward thee openly.

    Matthew 6:6

Section 10

CHURCH GROWTH THROUGH A GROUP OF BRANCH CHURCHES

Chapter 25

Church Growth through a United Group of Branch Churches U.G.B.C.

A United Group of Branch Churches UGBC

Traditionally, church growth is achieved through the swelling up of a single church until it seats thousands and thousands of people. However, there is another way to achieve church growth in our modern and complex world.

Through a network of several churches in different locations, you can achieve the same numbers as you would with a single huge church.

You can achieve church growth by setting up a united group of branch churches (UGBC) that are related and considered as one big family. This united group of churches would be the same church but in different locations. This group of branch churches will function as one unit with one team of leaders and pastors managing the church in different locations.

This group of churches will also function as one financial unit with incomes from the different locations. The financial capabilities of this united group of branch churches will be far greater than any single church.

Independent Mission Branch Churches (IMBC)

This united group of churches is in sharp contrast to independent missions that are sent out from the church. Independent branch churches are not the same as "one church in different locations". They are "different" churches in different locations.

These independent mission branch churches have independent leaders and independent financial systems.

They do not depend on each other for anything.

Independent mission churches may remit a percentage of its income to the headquarters.

The pastors of these churches have their own visions and dreams of what they want to do.

The pastors of these independent mission churches do not relate closely to the parent church.

Advantages of Having a United Group of Branch Churches (UGBC)

1. History has proved that united groups of branch churches are very often the most stable and established congregations everywhere. These networks of churches are sometimes called denominations. There are several well-known networks of churches in the world today.

    A united group of churches may be the way God wants to grow your church.

2. Belonging to a network of churches sometimes eliminates the instability that characterizes young independent churches. The institutional stagnation in a denomination may be a lesser evil compared to the advantages that come from belonging to a group of related churches.

3. In a network of branch churches, there are tried and tested principles that are passed on to sister churches.

4. In a united group of churches the good name serves as publicity and attracts people to the church. This name becomes like a franchise and serves as a powerful asset. The good name of a network of churches also has spiritual significance.

5. In a network of churches, trained members benefit from an established and respected system of pastoral training.

6. Members of a network of churches benefit from each other financially. You are not likely to get financial support from outside your network. Through a system of brotherly interdependence, churches are able to accomplish a lot.

7. Church members readily flow between churches belonging to a united group of branch churches. The network of churches is able to keep members within the fold. This enhances church growth.

8. Churches within a network of churches easily benefit from anointed senior ministers of that network.

9. Pastors within the network of churches can receive fatherly counsel and encouragement from seniors. Pastors of independent churches are usually suspicious and wary of external ministers who parade as fathers. There is little trust because independent churches often compete with one another rather than support each other.

10. Churches within a network operate under a particular spiritual covering. The same anointing runs through the entire network because it is really one church.

Principles for Operating a United Group of Branch Churches (UGBC)

1. **It is important to distinguish between independent mission branch churches (IMBC) and a united group of branch churches (UGBC) before you start branching out.**

    It is important to define and describe what exactly you are planning from the outset. If you fail to define these things from the beginning you will have lots of confusion and rebellion.

You must make the following points very clear before starting a united group of branch churches (UGBC):

a) That branch churches are not independent and will be continually monitored and governed by the headquarters.

b) That the mother church's finances will start the church and support it fully.

c). That income will flow into a central fund and ministers are paid from a central fund.

d) That all the needs of the branch churches and the headquarters will be met by the united group branch churches.

2. **Let the pastors and the congregations understand that it is the same church but in different locations. This means that congregation members are free to move from one location to another.**

3. **Set up an administration which monitors the attendance and finances of every member of the group of churches.**

Administer the finances of all the churches centrally; paying expenses and managing the bills centrally so that those who have more do not waste anything and those who have less do not suffer. "As it is written, He that had gathered much had nothing over; and he that had gathered little had no lack. (2 Corinthians 8:15).

This does not mean that all the money has to physically move to one place. The money does not have to move to one geographical location, but decisions concerning the money must be taken centrally.

A good church administration will manage the churches that have been created. To be a good administrator, you must have a good knowledge of secular issues.

Church administration requires a combination of the power of God and the wisdom of God. Without good church administration everything that you build will eventually collapse. You need to master church administration otherwise your ministry will be likened to a rocket that shoots off and falls apart shortly after takeoff.

But unto them which are called, both Jews and Greeks, Christ the power of God, and the wisdom of God.
1 Corinthians 1:24

4. **Maintain your leadership over the United Group of Branch Churches (UGBC).**

Churches and branches will be established by teaching and training the pastors constantly and requiring them to come for certain meetings and to meet certain standards.

5. **Let the church function as one large body (UGBC).**

The church in different locations will share its finances. This means that the money one church has belongs to all the other churches.

6. **Let the church function as one large body in different locations with shared leadership.**

Shared leadership means that pastors can be transferred from one location to another without destabilizing anything.

7. **Do not allow the branch pastors or branch churches to develop individualized visions.**

Their vision should be the vision of the UGBC group of churches in different locations.

8. **Study loyalty and teach extensively on loyalty.**

Fight independent-minded pastors who want to separate themselves and do something on their own. Such independent-minded people destroy the concept of the united group of branches (UGBC).

Loyalty is essential for maintaining a network of churches. The churches you will plant will not be in the same location. It is therefore necessary to teach people to be loyal wherever they are situated.

I once heard of someone criticizing me for teaching on loyalty.

He said, "Why should you teach on loyalty and disloyalty?"

He went on to say that it was not necessary to teach on loyalty because people will be inspired to loyalty by your good leadership.

I was not surprised that this dear critic of mine had never planted a single branch. It is amazing how people criticize something they have never done before.

On another occasion, a dear pastor criticized me for teaching on loyalty. However when his church split, he became an avid reader of my books and even promoted them to other ministers.

Loyalty is the subject which must be taught until the culture of faithfulness and loyalty is established in the UGBC.

9. **Be loyal to the branch pastors and churches so that they do not have any good reason or basis to separate themselves from you.**

   Show interest in and develop the branch churches so that your neglect of them does not become the reason for them to break away and separate themselves.

10. **Encourage the same teachings and books to be taught in the whole group of churches.**

    Conduct special programmes in the different branch churches to establish them.

11. **Let the entire group of churches remain connected through the internet.**

12. **Let the entire group of churches stay connected by having the same paraphernalia in every church; using the same offering baskets, banners, signboards.**

Laws for Managing a United Group of Branch Churches (UGBC)

Managing a network of churches is different from pastoring a single church. Pastoring a network of churches requires the development of a complex system of management. The laws for managing a complex network of churches are:

1. **Know:** Know what is going on in the different churches.

   This is done by developing a system in which reports are sent regularly to the headquarters. Weekly or monthly reports must contain vital information about the churches that you have established. This should include:

   i. The real attendance

   ii. What is preached and who preaches

   iii. The income of the church for the week.

2. **Communicate:** Communicate regularly to maintain a spirit of loyalty and togetherness in the family of churches.

   Reports must be sent to the headquarters by the most convenient method e.g. email, letter, fax, courier or by hand. Gradually, a well-controlled and fully- monitored system becomes established.

   The information must be used for taking decisions about churches and pastors.

3. **Influence:** Influence what is going on in the different churches.

   Influence what is going on by having frequent meetings with all the pastors and leaders. Meetings with the leaders are more important than meetings with the church itself.

4. **Encourage:** Churches that are part of the network need a lot of encouragement.

Pastors and churches greatly benefit from frequent visits by seasoned ministers.

5.   **Teach:** To maintain a spirit of loyalty and togetherness in the network.

It is important to teach on the advantages of belonging to the network.

Section 11

CHURCH GROWTH
AND ANAGKAZO

Chapter 26

Anagkazo, Biazo and *Anaideia*:
The Keys for Advancement

... Go out into the highways and hedges, and compel [anagkazo] them to come in, that my house may be filled.

Luke 14:23

What Is Anagkazo?

*A**nagkazo** simply means "to compel". It also means to necessitate, to drive, and to constrain* by all means such as *force, threats, persuasion* and *entreaties*.

Sometimes we need to go back to the Greek in order to understand the original meanings of some Bible words. You see, the New Testament was translated from the Greek language and the Old Testament from the Hebrew language. *Anagkazo* is the Greek word that is translated "to compel".

There is another closely related Greek word, *"Biazo"*.

What Is *Biazo*?

Biazo is a Greek word found in Matthew 11 that means *"to use force"* or *"to force one's way into a thing"*. This is a quality I find lacking in Christian circles. We are forceful about everything else, except God's work. We are forceful about our jobs, our girlfriends, our marriages and our future. But when it comes to God's work we become like timid mice!

When I see commercials on television, I realize that there are groups of people who are very confident about what they have to offer. They are so confident that they boldly sing catchy songs about how good their product is.

Alcohol advertisers are some of the best in the business. We all know that beer and liquor are killers and destroyers of young people. Alcohol has broken up more homes, destroyed more marriages, caused more car accidents, and started more wars and fights than anything else in the world. Yet, it is advertised and promoted constantly.

Beer is the cause of many accidents, leading to the deaths of countless numbers of people. And yet there are smiling people on television, telling us that it is the "power" we need. These commercials are being forced down our throats. We are being forced to believe things that are not true.

Even though beer is the "devil in solution" we are being compelled to believe otherwise.

When I think of the forcefulness of people who want to make money at all costs, I realize that Christians have a better reason to be forceful. Why then is it that we Christians behave like lame ducks, toothless dogs and helpless sparrows?

I believe that the revelation of *anagkazo* and *biazo* can change that. *Biazo* means to force one's way into a thing. If Christianity is going to spread we are going to have to be a lot more forceful than we are.

Whether it is making money, spreading a false religion or selling deadly products, the world is forceful about it. That is why I am teaching Christians to be biblically forceful.

What Is *Anaideia*?

Another related Greek word I want us to study is the word *Anaideia*. Anaideia is a Greek word that is used only once in the Bible. It means *"to be shameless"*. In the eleventh chapter of Luke, we learn of a man who exhibited shamelessness in his relationship with God.

I say unto you, Though he will not rise and give him, because he is his friend, yet because of his importunity

[anaideia] he will rise and give him as many as he needeth.

Luke 11:8

In 1982, I was admitted to the University of Ghana, the premier university in my country, Ghana. I cautiously entered this new environment wondering what lay ahead. One of the first things that struck me was the shamelessness of unbelievers.

The Kissing Students

I remember one of the first times I walked into Volta Hall, the ladies' hall. When I got to the staircase that led up to the first and second floors, there was a young man and a girl engaged in a prolonged embrace and kiss. I know that in some places this might not look strange. However it looked strange to me.

This couple continued in their long embrace and intimate kissing as we passed by them. They could not care less about who saw them! They were not moved! They were shameless! Perhaps they felt they were in love.

When we got upstairs, I told my friends, "It seems people around here are not ashamed of what they're doing."

Then I asked, "Why are we ashamed of what we believe in?

Why are we ashamed of the Gospel?

Why do we go around like timid mice that don't have anything to offer?"

The Spirit of the Lord rose up within me and I said, "If they are not ashamed of their immoral lives, I'm not going to be ashamed of the Gospel."

For I am not ashamed of the gospel of Christ...

Romans 1:16

It is amazing to see homosexuals boldly speak of their abnormal lifestyles. They come on television and speak confidently about the anomaly of anal intercourse. These people forcefully demonstrate for their rights. How come Christians are so quiet when it comes to speaking God's Word?

Many Christians sit in their offices and allow their unbeliever colleagues to shamelessly speak of their evil deeds. The sinners around us dominate the discussions with unwholesome words.

The Apostle Paul practised anaideia. Remember, it was Paul who said, "We are not ashamed of the Gospel."

Many Christians are genuine and have a real message to impart. But for a message to have any impact, it must be compelling. It must drive the listener to change! The message of the Lord Jesus Christ must persuade the unsaved to make a decision for Christ. It is so important for us to catch the message of *Anagkazo*, *Biazo* and *Anaideia*.

Chapter 27

Why *Anagkazo* is Important for Church Growth

In the fourteenth chapter of Luke, we read a familiar story where Jesus told of an important person who held a party for his friends. I want you to read this whole portion of Scripture so that you will be familiar with the story.

> **Then said he unto him, A certain man made a great supper, and bade many: And sent his servant at supper time to say to them that were bidden, Come; for all things are now ready.**
>
> **And they all with one consent began to make excuse. The first said unto him, I have bought a piece of ground, and I must needs go and see it: I pray thee have me excused.**
>
> **And another said, I have bought five yoke of oxen, and I go to prove them: I pray thee have me excused. And another said, I have married a wife, and therefore I cannot come.**
>
> **So that servant came, and shewed his lord these things. Then the master of the house being angry said to his servant, Go out quickly into the streets and lanes of the city, and bring in hither the poor, and the maimed, and the halt, and the blind. And the servant said, Lord, it is done as thou hast commanded, and yet there is room.**
>
> **And the lord said unto the servant, Go out into the highways and hedges, and compel [anagkazo] them to come in, that my house may be filled. For I say unto you, That none of those men which were bidden shall taste of my supper.**
>
> **Luke 14:16-24**

This man had the unfortunate experience of spending a lot of money on a big party, inviting important people, only to find out that most of them wouldn't come. This man was very surprised about their rejection of his invitation. He became angry as he listened to the excuses of those he had invited. In his anger, he decided to invite anybody he found on the street.

Imagine having a party with people you don't even know!

Unfortunately, at that time of the night, there were not so many people around. Even after inviting those on the street, his party was relatively unattended. He then decided to invite the sick, the blind and the handicapped. Imagine that! What an unusual selection of partygoers! His party was full of the nonentities and the down-and-outs of society.

Growth through *Anagkazo*

I believe this story is symbolic of the Lord Jesus sending us out to invite people to Him. It is also symbolic of pastors sending out their members to evangelize the world. I have discovered that every time I embark on evangelizing the world (inviting many people to a great supper), I encounter the same things that this man encountered. However, I believe this man was a success. In spite of everything, he had his party and his house was full of guests. It might not have turned out the way he initially wanted, but he had his party anyway.

You see, God is sending out His church to invite the whole world to know Christ. Unfortunately, many of those who are invited do not respond. The Jews were the first to be invited to know the Lord. But they rejected Christ and the Gospel moved on to the Gentiles.

Many of the elite, who live in large urban centres, hear the Gospel on television and in church. However, they do not receive the message but rather criticize preachers. Again, the Gospel is passed on to the poor and non-elite in villages. They willingly receive the Word because they have no other hope but God.

1. *Anagkazo* **is important because only a certain type of evangelism will lead to church growth.**

People are not going to be convinced or compelled to know God through our little church games. Our "Mickey Mouse" church programmes and bazaars will not go very far in today's world. We must go out there and drive them to God.

2. *Anagkazo* **is important because the people that will fill our empty churches are not in places where they can receive bourgeoisie invitation cards.**

If people are going to be touched with the Gospel, a new strategy of going to the gutters, highways and the bushes must be employed. Sitting in church and inviting people has long been an unworkable strategy for church growth.

3. **Dear pastor, without** *anagkazo*, **your church is going to be empty.**

Please remember that if this man had not employed the strategy of *anagkazo* he would have had an empty house. Remember this, "A pastor without *anagkazo* will have an empty church."

4. **Without anagkazo, many churches are going to die a natural death.**

What you must realize is that the membership of a church is very fluid. Many people come and many people leave. If you don't have more people coming in than those you are losing, your church will begin to die. If you don't want your church to close down, you must do what Jesus instructed – go out and practise anagkazo.

5. **Life is becoming more hectic and people are becoming more busy in the twenty-first century.**

Busy working people are going to have more and more excuses. The strategy of anagkazo will help you to overcome these excuses. Through your new driving and forceful attitude you will bring many people to Christ and to church.

Chapter 28

How to Use *Anagkazo* to Induce Church Growth

1. Use *anagkazo* to prepare a great supper.

Anyone who wants church growth must prepare for it. Most Christian outreaches are not successful unless there is a lot of preparation. Ask yourself how much preparation has gone into anything you do. If there is a lot of preparation there is usually a lot of success. Crusades, church growth, outreaches depend on your preparation. This anagkazo man prepared for his great programme.

Being in the ministry has not happened without thousands of hours of preparation. Sermons I preached to ten people some years ago are the same sermons I am preaching to thousands today.

Preaching to a small group of ten people was part of God's preparation for me. If you want God to use you mightily, you must start preparing now! Take every opportunity you have to do something useful in the church.

Years ago, I remember playing the drums and the piano in my church. Though I didn't know it at the time, that was part of my preparation for ministry. Today, I know a lot about music and musical equipment. I can discuss intelligently, all details that concern music, worship and expensive equipment. My experience with the music department has been a valuable asset to me.

2. Use *anagkazo* to influence many people.

You will notice that this man in Luke 14 held a great supper and invited many people. One of the primary reasons churches do not grow is because Christians keep to themselves. You cannot keep to yourself if you want to be an effective witness for the Lord Jesus Christ.

When you sit on a bus, you can decide to be friendly to those nearby. Begin talking to the people around you. I always try to share the Gospel with people around me. I always have some Good News about Jesus. He has saved me and set me free.

During my second year in medical school, we lived on the beautiful Legon campus. We were transported daily to the other side of town where a teaching hospital was located. This involved a one-hour bus drive from one end of town to the other.

Balloons and Condoms

I remember one day as I sat in the bus, I watched some senior colleagues take out condoms, blow them into balloons and fly them in the bus. As these students shouted and laughed over their lewd jokes, I realized how confident they were in what they were doing.

We the Christians sat timidly in the bus, trying to concentrate on our books.

That day, I decided not to keep to myself. I got the attention of everyone on the bus and began to preach. Although preaching on the bus later became quite common, at that time it was unusual. Some of the students were angry and others were bored. Some looked out of the window in disapproval but I preached on! I decided not to keep to myself anymore. I decided to be like the man in Luke 14.

Clapping on the London Bus

An *anagkazo* person does not keep to himself. I once lived in London for a period of time. I felt stifled by the stiff atmosphere in England. I was used to preaching anywhere and everywhere. But in England I couldn't easily relate to the people around. Everyone seemed so unfriendly and uninterested.

One day, while sitting upstairs in a double-decker bus, the spirit of *anagkazo* rose up in me and I said to myself, "I can't keep it to myself any longer."

I rose to my feet and to the surprise of everyone on the bus, I began to clap my hands to get their attention. I tell you, I may have looked bold on the outside, but I was quite scared on the inside.

There were all sorts of murderous looking characters on the bus. But I maintained my cool and delivered a complete Gospel sermon.

The bus was quiet for a few minutes as they listened to this young madman preach. I took my seat after preaching and got off at the next stop. One gentleman, who got off the bus with me said to me, "I admire your courage! But I don't think you got very far." Whether I got very far or not is not what matters. What is important is that I preached the Word. And the Word always accomplishes something when it is preached. ...my word be that goeth forth out of my mouth... it shall accomplish that which I please..." (Isaiah 55:11)

3. Use *anagkazo* and never cancel your service. Anyone practising *anagkazo* is not prepared to cancel his service.

Every pastor, in going through the normal processes of church growth, will experience highs and lows. But a pastor with the spirit of *anagkazo* will never cancel his church service. He will decide to press on no matter how many people attend.

One of my pastors told me how only one person attended church on a particular Sunday. He said that he had never felt so low. However, he managed to preach to that one soul and do his best for the Lord.

Anagkazo in the Community

I remember there was a time we had a very low attendance for one of our services. The Lord told me to do what this man in Luke 14 did: "Go out there and invite the community to church."

I said, "How can I do that on a Sunday?"

The Lord replied, "You do it, and you will be blessed."

I continued arguing with the Lord, "What will our Sunday morning visitors think? We will drive away people from the church."

However, the Lord insisted, "Go out and compel them to come in."

I obeyed the Lord.

I announced to the church that we were going to stop the service, go out into the community and invite them.

I said, "We are going to go out to the community to bring them in."

I announced, "This is not a gentle invitation. Every single one of you must hold the hand of someone you see out there. Physically bring them into the church building."

Some were taken aback. But we did it! And we brought in hundreds of "un-churched" dwellers of the community. That day we had several people giving their lives to Christ. We did this on numerous occasions and over a period, that particular service increased in size dramatically. I was not prepared to close down my service because of a low attendance. That is what any pastor with the spirit of *anagkazo* is prepared to do.

4. Use *anagkazo* to prevent having empty halls.

A pastor working with the spirit of anagkazo is not prepared to have an empty church service. Many years ago, as a medical student, the Lord asked me to start a church. I had no members in my church. Not even one soul to preach to! But I was not prepared to have an empty church.

Anagkazo and the Dawn Broadcast

I was still a student when the Holy Spirit directed me to the nursing students' hostel. I remember that very first day. It was around 5 a.m. and still dark. Standing outside the hostel, I clapped my hands and woke them up. They might have been surprised but that didn't bother me. I preached to them about Jesus. After I had finished I did something very bold. I said to them, "If you want to give your lives to Christ, change out of your night clothes, wear something decent and come downstairs. We want to talk to you about Christ."

That morning several young ladies gave their hearts to God. Up to this day, many of them are still members of my church.

Preaching at dawn to people in their beds has been one of my favourite methods of implementing this principle of anagkazo. One morning, I preached at the hostel of public health nurses. A lady threw down a note saying she was a backslider and needed help. She wanted us to speak with her. That morning we ministered to her and God delivered her. She has been a faithful member of our church for the last ten years.

Although I started out with an empty classroom, it soon became filled with nurses who had given their lives to Christ from my *anagkazo* dawn broadcasts.

Dear reader, I want you to understand something; I did not inherit a church from anyone. I have often gone to places where I knew no one, and no one knew me. I have had to go out and win souls, driving and persuading people to the Lord, until the room was full.

5. Use *anagkazo* to overcome people's excuses.

Many people are full of excuses. The man in the story listened to three amazing excuses for not attending his party. However, he was not impressed by any of them.

The first excuse was about testing oxen in the night. Everyone knows that no one tests oxen at that time of the night.

The second excuse was about somebody who had just gotten married. But we all know that a dinner would have been a nice outing for a newly-wed couple.

The third excuse was about going to see some land in the night. Let me ask you a question. Would you not assess a piece of land before you buy it? How could you inspect a piece of land in the night? Would you even see it clearly? Yet somebody was using this as an excuse for not attending the party.

Any good minister, who wants to reach people, must not be overwhelmed by people's excuses. He must learn to overcome people's excuses.

Even as you minister the Word of God, people form excuses in their minds. They develop reasons why they will not obey the Word. Every good preacher must learn to preach against people's excuses and ideas. Jesus spoke directly against the people's reasoning and excuses. And they knew it!

... for they perceived that he had spoken this parable against them.

Luke 20:19

Many excuses cannot be substantiated. A good minister must learn to see through the emptiness of excuses. I spoke to one friend, inviting him to church. He in turn spoke about how the time was not convenient and how he had quite a distance to travel.

I said to him, "You are a successful businessman. Everything you want to do, you do. You travel. You get up early everyday. You even have time to visit your girlfriend who lives a few hundred kilometres away. How come you have no time for God?"

I told him, "If you really want to do something you can do it."

Some people do not pay their tithes because they claim they have no money. Watch how much money they spend on other things. You will realize that the problem is not a lack of money, but the spirit of greed.

6. Use *anagkazo* to overcome people's lies.

I remember once, one of my pastors did some fundraising in a branch church.

During the fundraising, the pastor asked for those who would like to give some money for the purchase of church instruments.

A husband who happened to be a foreigner was prepared to give a donation. Just as his hand was going up, his wife pulled his hand down. She thought the pastor hadn't noticed.

After the service, the lady approached the pastor and said, "You know, the reason why we didn't give any money during the fundraising was because my foreign husband didn't want to give.

She continued, "You know how these foreigners are. They are so stingy."

But that was a lie. It was she who did not want to give anything.

Finally she promised the pastor, "I will see what we can do. I am sure we will be able to help."

All pastors must learn to overcome the lies and excuses of the people we lead.

7.   Use *anagkazo* to make a way.

What differentiates the successful from the unsuccessful is the ability to overcome excuses. Notice that the man in Luke 14 was not moved by any of the excuses and reasons given. He made a way out of every circumstance that was produced by the unwilling guests.

I believe in one thing: If you really want to do something you make a way, if you do not want to do something you make an excuse.

They Came to Party

I recall when many young people were unwilling to come to church. The young men especially, made all sorts of excuses. The spirit of anagkazo rose up in me and I said, "If they will not come to church, let us have parties for them."

We organized a party for the young people in one area of the city. We made invitation cards and distributed them to the youth in the community. They were very happy and said to themselves, "This is another opportunity to jam."

I remember that evening in particular, we played upbeat Christian music and danced with the unbelievers. One of them told me later that he wondered why they were not being served with beer. At a point in the party, we switched to slower music and stated we had an announcement to make.

By that time, many of the hardened unbelievers were sitting around. To their surprise, I got up and preached the Gospel to them. They were surprised but they still gave their lives to Christ. Many were born again that night.

I have pastors in the church who were saved during some of these surprise evangelistic parties. The Bible says by all means, "save some".

Anagkazo means to compel and to drive people to God. An anagkazo person is not moved by unfavourable circumstances. We were not moved by the fact that these young men did not want to attend church. We made a way around that! Learn to make a way where there's no way. Find a way to overcome every excuse that people place before you.

8.   Use *anagkazo* to go out of your usual circle of friends.

Everyone has a circle of friends. The usual thing is to stay within your circle of friends and acquaintances. However, anyone who wants to be used by God must move out of this regular group. You will notice that the anagkazo man in this story was forced to move out of his normal circle of friends. This is a reality that we must face if we want to please God!

I Had My Circle

I had a group of friends I grew up with in Accra. A sort of elitist company made up of the children of foreigners and other bourgeoisie. As a child I travelled first class on intercontinental flights and interacted mainly with the so-called upper echelon of society. I stayed in international cities with my father. My hobbies were swimming and horse riding and horse racing. There were just a few people who had such pastimes.

However, there were hardly any Christians in these circles. When I got born again, I found myself moving out of this circle into a very different group. I moved out into better company, different from what I knew.

The fact is, in order to please God I could not spend a lot of time in those circles anymore. There were simply no believers in that group. If you want to please God you will have to move out of your circle and get to know other groups of people.

I know that the rich man in this story would not normally fellowship with people who live in hedges or who stand on highways.

I know that the rich man in this story would not normally interact with cripples, the blind and the disabled. However, in order to achieve church growth he had to interact with people of other social backgrounds.

The Nice Little Fellowship Must Grow

I remember in 1984 when I was the leader of a nice fellowship at the university.

We loved each other dearly and were good company for one another (actually, I found my wife in that group). Many of the people that I knew in that little group are still my bosom friends up to this day. However, the Spirit of God impressed upon me to move out of our little group and to go to people we didn't know.

I remember some people were not in favour of expanding our nice little clique.

"If you bring in more people, we will lose something," they said. "There's something about a small fellowship. It's nice to be petite. It's a cute little family."

But I led this group into one outreach after another, driving and necessitating people to come to the Lord. I was never tired of preaching. People are not tired of sinning, why should you be tired of spreading the gospel?

155

During the second year of the medical school (which by the way is the most difficult year), I led this group in dawn broadcasts every Saturday morning. Everyone knew about us. They were used to our voices that rang out loud and clear every Saturday morning.

"Thank God for our nice little fellowship," I said. "But we have to go out there and win souls." We must move out of our little circle.

After awhile, unbelievers are no longer impressed with our sermons. If you do not rise up with a new approach, a new *anagkazo* method, your message will lose its punch.

As we continued preaching at dawn, I realized that people just turned over in their beds and ignored us. I said to myself, "Our messages are no longer driving people to the Lord."

But the Spirit of the Lord gave me a bright idea.

Knock on Their Doors!

Since the people were now so used to our voices, we needed to do something new. I decided to send out a group to stand outside the doors of their rooms.

I told the preacher for the morning, "When you get to the altar call, we will start knocking on their doors."

I told him, "Tell the people who are listening to you that they are going to hear a knock on their door. If they want to accept Christ they should open up and we will come in and lead them to the Lord."

The preacher followed my instructions. Suddenly, those who were ignoring us had to pay attention. We were knocking on their doors at 5 a.m.! Believe me, many were gloriously born again during those morning broadcasts.

Salvation for the Mocker

I vividly remember one brother in particular; He would laugh at Christians as they spoke in tongues. He made fun of the gift of speaking in tongues. This is someone who would get drunk and lie by one of the many ponds scattered around the beautiful campus of the University of Ghana. That morning as my friend the evangelist preached and said, "Perhaps you are hearing a knock on your door. If you want to be born again open your door and someone will come in and lead you to the Lord", I happened to knock on the door of this young man.

I was surprised when he opened the door and welcomed us in. He said, "I knew you would come here. Today is my day!" We prayed with him and he gave his heart to the Lord that very morning. To this day, this man is serving the Lord. I give glory to God for all the people that have been born again as we have forcefully moved out to speak the Word. Anagkazo works!

9.   Use *anagkazo* until there is no more room in your church.

   ...and yet there is room.

Luke 14:22

A song that I love goes like this: *There's room at the cross for you. There's room at the cross for you. Though millions have come, there's still room for one. There's room at the cross for you.*

Do not be satisfied as long as there is room in your church. The man in this story sent out his servants simply because there was room.

I believe that every church should arrange more chairs than the people who actually come. The presence of empty pews should motivate the pastor to reach out until the house is full. The whole essence of church growth is to have a full church.

   ...compel [anagkazo] them to come in, that my house may be filled.

Luke 14:23

Evangelism is directly related to church growth. All our efforts to lead people to the Lord should bear fruit. We must see our efforts filling church buildings.

Whatever the case, a minister must see that there is room at the cross for one more soul. I believe that if we have this mind, God will use us to fill the church.

I have never been satisfied with the size of my church. When we had ten people, I wanted twenty. When we had fifty, I dreamed of a hundred. When God gave me one hundred people, I thought to myself, "What would it be like if I had five hundred people?" When the church was numbered in the hundreds, I thought, "What would it be like if we had thousands?"

I think a pastor will get tired of preaching to the same few people after awhile. We must be motivated to have a fuller house. These words keep ringing in my soul, "That my house may be filled!" "That my house may be filled!" Dear Pastor, never forget that there is still room at the cross.

Chapter 29

How *Anaideia* and *Biazo* Cause Church Growth

A naideia and *biazo* are the keys to church growth. Evangelism is the key to getting new people to join your church. Without biazo and anaideia you will not have the strength to evangelise.

Biazo

Verily I say unto you, among them that are born of women there hath not risen a greater than John the Baptist: notwithstanding he that is least in the kingdom of heaven is greater than he. And from the days of John the Baptist until now the kingdom of heaven suffereth violence, and the violent [biazo] take it by force.

Matthew 11:11,12

Multitudes of non-Christians are hurtling down a broad street to Hell. They sing, they dance, and they wine and dine. They do not give a hoot about the Gospel we preach! Many of us Christians live in our nice little world where we are oblivious to the reality of sinners going to Hell.

I once worked as a sub-intern at the mortuary of the largest hospital in Ghana. Something struck me that I want to share with you. Every few minutes a car would park outside the mortuary. In that car was the body of a man sprawled in the back seat, or even sometimes in the boot (trunk).

I would stand at the main door of the mortuary as people brought in their loved ones and relatives who had died at home or on the street. These people were so sad and shaken. You must understand that only a few hours earlier they had been talking to a living person who was now gone forever. They were bringing their loved one to a fridge.

I noticed that there did not seem to be any particular time of the day when dead people were brought to this mortuary. As I stood there, God showed me that people were dying across the city all the time. Death is not reserved for early mornings or late nights. It happens anytime and anywhere.

A person who has never stood at the door of a mortuary will not know how common death is. How frequently people depart for eternity! Just as the Lord spoke to his prophets when they saw certain things, the Lord spoke to me when I stood at that door. He asked, "How many of these people do you think were saved?"

"I died for them; I gave up my life for them, but are they saved?"

Listen to me Christian friend. Our church bazaars, weddings, fellowships and nice choirs are not enough to win the multitudes to Christ. People are hurtling down the road of destruction. They do not even know that they are going to Hell.

They Heard the Music

This reminds me of the Second World War in which the prisoners were taken to large camps. They were stripped of their clothes and herded into huge gas chambers. As they filed in, their captors would play beautiful music for the prisoners. They heard the music. How soothing and refreshing it must have sounded. "Surely nothing evil is going to happen to us," they thought. Little did they know that they were about to be slaughtered by the same people who were playing the music.

This is the lot of unbelievers today. They hear the music of the devil. The melodies and lullabies of this present world charm them. Because of these things, they do not know that they are walking to their own destruction. "...as an ox goeth to the slaughter..." (Proverbs 7:22).

In Matthew 11:12, the Bible tells us that the violent take the kingdom of God by force. What does this mean?

The Twentieth Century New Testament puts it this way, ... **men using force have been seizing it**...

The William's Translation says, ...**men are seizing it as a precious prize...**

The Goodspeed translation says, ...**Men have been taking the kingdom of heaven by storm**...

The Weymouth translation says, ...**the kingdom of God has been enduring violent assault**...

All these Scriptures tell us one thing. Gentle words, nice songs, lame sermons and docile choirs cannot help much in this indifferent and uninterested world. People don't want to know. They are deceived.

Church Games Will Not Help

They don't care whether Jesus comes today or tomorrow. "Leave me alone," they say. "To Hell with this church business of yours."

That is why we need what the Bible calls *Biazo*. *Biazo* means to use force and to force one's way into a thing. Many people are blinded by the devil. We must open their eyes to the realities of Heaven and Hell.

...the god of this world hath blinded the minds of them...

2 Corinthians 4:4

Apostle Paul did not only give nice sermons. He was actively involved in turning the heads and opening the eyes of unbelievers.

I always know when people are ignoring the message. But I don't want anybody to ignore this important message – I must turn their heads and open their eyes. One particular morning, my group in the university found ourselves in a hall, preaching.

When we have city-wide crusades, I stand on the platform and command my church members to go out into the community. We don't wait for them to come to us; we go out there and bring them from their homes.

One day, we even went to a "Red Light District" and brought a group of prostitutes to the crusade. I was very happy to see these prostitutes coming to the altar to give their lives to the Lord. You see, if we hadn't forced these women out of their "work places" and to the crusade, they would never have been saved. Most prostitutes do not go to church. They would have just gone about their daily routine. We would have ended up preaching to ourselves.

Christian friends, let's stop playing games. If we are going to preach the Gospel, let's not preach to ourselves. Let's go out there and drive them in (*anagkazo* and *biazo*) to the Lord.

Anaideia

I say unto you, Though he will not rise and give him, because he is his friend, yet because of his importunity [anaideia] he will rise and give him as many as he needeth.

Luke 11:8

In Luke 11, Jesus told us a story of a man who needed three loaves of bread. This man buried his shame and embarrassment and went to his friend's house at a very odd hour. The master of the house was woken up.

He might have shouted, "What is happening? Are there some armed robbers here? Is there a fire? What is going on outside?" The servant of the house probably replied, "It's the neighbour. He says he wants some bread for his visitors."

Dear Christian friend, most of us would not disturb even our best friends at midnight. How much more to ask for something trivial like bread!

But Jesus' message here is very simple. If you are ashamed to press for certain things, you will never achieve them. If you are shameless in trying to achieve church growth you will accomplish things that others will only dream about! God has shown me that people who are very concerned about their public image cannot achieve much for God.

Are You Ashamed to Pursue Church Growth?

It takes anaideia, shamelessness, to start a church. When I discussed with my friend the idea of starting a church, I remember he looked at me in amazement. He said, "What if people don't come to the church? We will be so embarrassed. People in town will hear that we tried to start a church that didn't work."

By starting a church, I don't mean to break away with a large segment of someone else's ministry. I am talking about moving into a room that has two or three people and preaching to them. It takes shamelessness to tell these few people that they are now in a great church. If you are not prepared to go through the shame and ridicule of standing in an empty room and looking odd, you will never achieve great things for God.

Are You Ashamed of Church Work?

One pastor told me he was afraid to do an altar call (inviting people to give their life to Christ). What if no one responds? Would you not feel ashamed? People will think that you are not anointed and that your message was not powerful enough. It is this very train-of-thought that keeps people away from powerful ministry.

One of my Elders called and told me that for the first time someone in the church had responded to her altar call. You see, she had been shamelessly doing altar calls with no one responding. But with *anaideia* (shamelessness and persistence) she eventually had results!

Are You Ashamed of the Healing Ministry?

The shameless man, who asked for the bread, eventually accomplished his goal. I remember when I first began to pray for the sick. I was very worried about what people would think about me.

Many times whilst standing on stage, the devil would tell me, "Don't even bother to call out for testimonies; no one will be healed."

The devil told me, "Do not disgrace yourself any further. Just end the service here and send the people home."

But the Spirit of the Lord rose up within me and I said to myself, "I am not ashamed. If no one gets healed this time, I will do it again, and again, and again! One day, someone will get healed." I am glad to say that many have been healed.

After I had qualified from the medical school, I worked for one year as a medical doctor.

Are You Ashamed of Full-Time Ministry?

At a point, the Lord began to speak to me about entering full-time ministry. I argued with the Lord, "I will work and bring enough money to support the church."

I continued, "What will people think of me, leaving such a noble profession to enter such a controversial one." I told the Lord, "No one knows my church! And no one knows me!"

"Worst of all, what a shame it is for me to live off people's offerings."

"That's ridiculous! Why should people contribute their pennies for my upkeep? I find it degrading," I thought.

However, the Lord told me, "They that preach the Gospel must live off the Gospel."

Even so hath the Lord ordained that they which preach the gospel should live of the gospel.
1 Corinthians 9:14

I had to bury my pride as a doctor and shamelessly enter full-time ministry. Through the revelation of shamelessness (*anaideia*), I have gone far in ministry. I have achieved things, which no one ever thought would come out of me.

Anaideia (shamelessness) is the key you need to accomplish great things for God!

Section 12

CHURCH GROWTH AND
HARD LEADERSHIP

Chapter 30

Why You Must Become a Hard Leader to Have Church Growth

... I will liken him unto a wise man, which built his house upon a rock:

Matthew 7:24

The traditional picture of a pastor is of a soft, kind and understanding man who listens to all the problems of the congregation. This kind pastor is so loving and understanding of all the issues that are presented. He has time for everyone and he cares for everyone's children. He is gentle and friendly to everyone who wants to talk to him.

This is the picture that I also had of a pastor. I was therefore shocked when I heard from Dr David Yonggi Cho, (pastor of the largest church in the world) that to build a large church you need to be a very strong leader. I thought it was contradictory since the pastor was supposed to be a soft, gentle, caring man who loved the people with the love of the Lord.

What does hardness and strength of leadership have to do with pastoring large numbers of people? As time has gone by, however, I have found out for myself how important it is to be a strong and hard leader if you are to have church growth.

Indeed, this idea of strong, hard leadership for church growth is a totally biblical concept with many supporting Scriptures.

1. You must be a hard leader because you can only build a large house on a rock solid foundation.

You cannot build a big church on a soft leader. You need a hard leader upon whom you can build a huge ministry. The church is the house of God and equally needs a rock as its foundation.

You need a rock because the rain is going to fall, the floods are going to come and the winds are going to blow on the church you are building. If there is no hardness in the foundation there is no hope for the future.

> ...I will liken him unto a wise man, which built his house upon a rock:
> And the rain descended, and the floods came, and the winds blew, and beat upon that house; and it fell not: for it was founded upon a rock.
>
> Matthew 7:24-25

2. You must be a hard leader because Jesus Christ wanted Peter, the head of His church to be a hard rock.

He changed Peter's name into "the rock" because He knew that a hard person was needed to build the worldwide church. Jesus wanted Peter to be a hard leader, not easily moved around. You must also be a hard leader who is not easily moved around.

> And I say also unto thee, that thou art Peter, and upon this rock I will build my church; and the gates of hell shall not prevail against it.
>
> Matthew 16:18

3. You must be a hard leader because Jesus recommended John, the greatest prophet, for being a hard person.

People who are soft and wishy-washy do not head great ministries. A wishy-washy leader is someone lacking in decisiveness. He is without strength or character. Great ministries are often headed by hard leaders who are not moved by what people say but are moved by what God says.

John the Baptist could not be bothered by what people thought. He was not even bothered by what the king thought. He took no thought for his life as he rebuked the king for marrying his brother's wife. No wonder Jesus recommended him.

> And as they departed, Jesus began to say unto the multitudes concerning John, What went ye out into the wilderness to see? A reed shaken with the wind?

But what went ye out for to see? A man clothed in soft raiment? Behold, they that wear soft *clothing* are in kings' houses.
But what went ye out for to see? A prophet? Yea, I say unto you, and more than a prophet.

Matthew 11:9

4. You must be a hard leader because everything depends on the leader.

… smite the shepherd, and the sheep of the flock shall be scattered abroad.

Matthew 26:31

Everything depends on the shepherd. Everything depends on the leader. When the shepherd is down everyone goes down with him. A whole church cannot lean on something that is soft, weak and indecisive. Unstable, waffling and weak-kneed leaders have no place at the head of a large ministry. To be the captain of the ship means everybody's life depends on you. To be the pilot of a plane means everyone's life depends on you.

The Soft Pilot

I once watched a documentary of such a weak leader who was the pilot of a flight from Colombia to New York. He was asked to delay his landing because of air traffic at the airport. Can you believe that he flew his plane around in circles until he finally ran out of fuel and crashed the plane, killing many people?

Of course, an investigation was launched into this terrible tragedy. The air crash investigation eventually ruled that this pilot had not put sufficient pressure on the air traffic control and had not impressed upon them strongly enough that he was running out of fuel.

That night this weak-kneed pilot killed many people, including himself, because he lacked the strength to impress upon air traffic control that he needed to land urgently.

He also lacked the strength to forcefully (and illegally, if necessary) land his plane when he knew that everyone was in grave danger.

This is what it is like to have a weak and soft person in charge of everything. This is why Jesus wanted Peter to be a rock. He wanted a hard person to be the head of His Church.

5. **You must be a hard leader because the head of the church, Jesus Christ, is a hard leader and He does not apologize for it.**

> Then he which had received the one talent came and said, Lord, I knew thee that thou art AN HARD MAN, reaping where thou hast not sown, and gathering where thou hast not strawed:
> And I was afraid, and went and hid thy talent in the earth: lo, there thou hast that is thine.
> His lord answered and said unto him, Thou wicked and slothful servant, THOU KNEWEST THAT I REAP WHERE I SOWED NOT, AND GATHER WHERE I HAVE NOT STRAWED:
> Thou oughtest therefore to have put my money to the exchangers, and *then* at my coming I should have received mine own with usury.
>
> Matthew 25:24-27

Jesus told us parables that illustrated His hardness as a leader. He made no apologies for this reality. In this parable, the servant accused their leader of being hard. "Thou art a hard man" they said. In their opinion, this hard leader had benefits they thought he didn't deserve. But the Lord did not deny that he was a hard man. In fact, he confirmed that he was as hard as they thought: reaping where he had not sown.

Dear friend, you will need to be as hard as our Lord if you are going to get anything done for the kingdom.

Chapter 31

The Hardness and the Decisions of a Mega Church Pastor

The hardness and decisions of a mega church pastor mark out the character of his leadership. A mega church pastor will need strength to drive the congregation forward into the Promised Land.

His strength will be revealed through the hard decisions that he takes and his ability to follow through with what he has decided.

I want to share with you a few of the decisions that a strong, hard pastor would probably have to take whilst building a large church.

1. **A pastor who is building a large church will have to take decisions to put the right people in the right places.**

If you go by what the majority think you can never be the pastor of a mega church. Joseph was chosen to be the prime minister and to have authority over the whole of Egypt. Can you imagine how the other departmental heads felt when this Israeli slave was made their boss?

And Pharaoh said unto Joseph, Forasmuch as God hath shewed thee all this, *there* is none so discreet and wise as thou art: Thou shalt be over my house, and according unto thy word shall all my people be ruled: only in the throne will I be greater than thou. And Pharaoh said unto Joseph, See, I have set thee over all the land of Egypt.

Genesis 41:39-41

2. **A pastor who is building a large church will have to rebuke people who are out of order in the church.**

If you cannot rebuke people who are out of order you cannot be the pastor of a mega church. People constantly step out of order. They want to see how strong you are. They want to see how far they can go. They want to see if you will address those uncomfortable issues. Everybody is watching to see how strong you can be.

> But he turned, and said unto Peter, Get thee behind me, Satan: thou art an offence unto me: for thou savourest not the things that be of God, but those that be of men.
>
> Matthew 16:23

3. A pastor who is building a large church will have to take the hard decisions not to allow his wife to lead him or guide him in the ministry.

Adam was guided by his wife into the chaos we now experience in the world. Abraham was guided by his wife into giving birth to Ishmael. In both cases the Bible uses the phrase, "And Adam/Abraham hearkened unto the voice of his wife...."

Ahab was guided into murder and stealing by his wife.

Ahab, like Adam and Abraham, allowed himself to be guided, influenced and prodded into evil.

Job, on the other hand, was pressurized by his wife to curse God. But Job would have none of it and called her a foolish woman! If you cannot reject erroneous influence coming from your own wife, you cannot be a mega church pastor.

A hard mega church pastor must be able to see foolishness in his wife when it surfaces. Your wife is not an angel and she is not God. She is just a human being like anyone else. If you can't distinguish the evil from the good, you cannot be a mega church pastor. You must be able to call your wife a foolish woman if she tells you to curse God and die!

> Then SAID HIS WIFE unto him, Dost thou still retain thine integrity? CURSE GOD, AND DIE. But he said unto her, Thou speakest as one of the foolish women speaketh. What? shall we receive good at the hand of God, and shall we not receive evil? In all this did not Job sin with his lips.
>
> Job 2:9-10

4. A pastor who is building a large church will have to take the hard decisions to keep his wife in her place.

A mega church pastor must ensure that his wife does not do anything to destroy the work of God. Michal's comments could have ended the praise and worship ministry of David. But David did not allow it. He would carry on his praise and worship ministry in spite of what his wife thought. He sharply rebuked her and disconnected from her! He continued his ministry of "abandoned praise and worship".

Today, we all sing those heart-felt psalms that came from a man who abandoned himself helplessly before his God.

When David returned home to bless his family, Michal came out to meet him and said in disgust, "How glorious the king of Israel looked today! He exposed himself to the servant girls like any indecent person might do!"

David retorted to Michal, "I was dancing before the Lord, who chose me above your father and his family! He appointed me as the leader of Israel, the people of the Lord. So I am willing to act like a fool in order to show my joy in the Lord.

Yes, and I am willing to look even more foolish than this, but I will be held in honor by the girls of whom you have spoken!

2 Samuel 6:20-22 (NLT)

5. A pastor who is building a large church will have to take the hard decisions to reach out and do evangelism.

It takes strength to lead the church out as an army. It takes strength to lead pampered Sunday Christians into the evangelistic mode. It takes strength to preach about the need for the Gospel to money-loving prosperity-seeking congregants.

Then tidings of these things came unto the ears of the church which was in Jerusalem: and they sent forth Barnabas, that he should go as far as Antioch. Who, when he came, and had seen the grace of God, was glad, and exhorted them all, that with purpose of heart they would cleave unto the Lord.

For he was a good man, and full of the Holy Ghost and of faith: and much people was added unto the Lord.

Acts 11:22-24

6. A pastor who is building a large church will have to take the hard decisions to send people out to start branches.

It is not easy to send people away. We love staying with the people we love and enjoying their company. But this is the very thing that will kill the growth of the church.

And when they had fasted and prayed, and laid their hands on them, they sent them away.

Acts 13:3

7. A pastor who is building a large church will have to take hard decisions to treat people differently.

It is not easy to relate to people according to God's gift. People always compare themselves with others. They ask, "What is this person doing and what am I doing? What is this person getting and what am I getting? Where is this person going and why am I not going?

Because leaders are afraid to treat people differently, they often keep the wrong people in the wrong places doing the wrong things.

Peter seeing him saith to Jesus, Lord, and what shall this man do? Jesus saith unto him, If I will that he tarry till I come, what is that to thee? Follow thou me.

John 21:21-22

8. A pastor who is building a large church will have to take the hard decision to build something.

Building involves a lot. Nehemiah suffered greatly because he decided to build the walls of Jerusalem. Building the house of God often involves fighting a spiritual war and building at the same time.

They which builded on the wall, and they that bare burdens, with those that laded, every one with one of his hands wrought in the work, and with the other hand held a weapon.

For the builders, every one had his sword girded by his side, and so builded. And he that sounded the trumpet was by me.

Nehemiah 4:17-18

9. A pastor who is building a large church will have to take hard decisions that make people sacrifice their money and their lives.

It is not easy to make people sacrifice their lives. It takes a hard commander to send people to their certain death.

Now when Jesus heard these things, he said unto him, yet lackest thou one thing: sell all that thou hast, and distribute unto the poor, and thou shalt have treasure in heaven: and come, follow me.

Luke 18:22

10. A pastor who is building a large church will have to take a decision to lead the people in hours of prayer.

It is not easy to lead people in long hours of prayer. It takes a hard leader to force the congregation to go through the discipline of long hours of prayer.

And he cometh unto the disciples, and findeth them asleep, and saith unto Peter, What, could ye not watch with me one hour?

Matthew 26:40

11. A pastor who is building a large church will have to take decisions to practise frugality in the church. It is not easy to be frugal. It is not easy to lead people in a frugal lifestyle. People rebel against hardships. If you are not a hard strong leader, you cannot lead your organization into frugality.

When they were filled, he said unto his disciples, Gather
up the fragments that remain, that nothing be lost.

John 6:12

12. A pastor who is building a large church will have to take decisions to lead the entire congregation in hard and difficult times of fasting.

Then the king and his nobles sent this decree throughout
the city: "No one, not even the animals, may eat or drink
anything at all.
Everyone is required to wear sackcloth and pray earnestly
to God. Everyone must turn from their evil ways and stop
all their violence.

Jonah 3:7-8 (NLT)

13. A pastor who is building a large church will have to take decisions to dismiss certain people and replace them with others.

And the king... set the royal crown upon her head, and
made her queen instead of Vashti.

Esther 2:17

14. A pastor who is building a large church will have to take the hard decision to make the people give him his due honour.

Many times a pastor has no one to say certain things for him
and he will have to say them himself. Learn to say the hard things
that you have to say if there is no one to say it for you.

I had to tell the church myself that I was a pastor. I had to
tell my church how to address me. On another occasion I had to
inform them that I was a Bishop.

And Elijah said unto her, Fear not; go and do as thou hast
said: but make me thereof a little cake first, and bring it
unto me, and after make for thee and for thy son.

1 Kings 17:13

Section 13

CHURCH GROWTH
AND COPYING

Chapter 32

The Art of Copying

Copying is the art of following a pattern or model until you have reproduced a good imitation of the original.

All successful pastors copied from someone else. Church growth is accomplished by pastors who are willing to copy from other pastors. There is no shame in copying from someone who has experienced what you need.

Copying may be a bad word to you, but copying is only bad when it is illegally done during examinations. Copying is the highest form of learning and is the God-given method of learning which babies and children use.

"Be an original," they say. But the reality is that everyone copied from someone else. Every great worship leader copied from some worship leader somewhere else. Every great evangelist copied from another evangelist. Every great man of God is a copy of some other man of God somewhere.

Every anointing is a copy of another anointing. The anointing that came on Peter, James and John was simply a copy of the anointing that was on Jesus their master. The anointing that was on Elisha was simply another of the same kind of what was on Elijah.

Recently, I was having breakfast in a hotel in an African country and here came along a famous Christian singer whose music and CDs are played all over the world. As we sat together, one of my pastors, asked him a question, "Who has influenced your music ministry?"

He answered, "Oh, Andre Crouch has been my greatest inspiration."

I immediately understood why this fellow was doing so well. He was simply a copy of someone else. He was proud to be another of the same kind.

I have noticed that all those who do well in any field, are those who closely follow after someone of the same kind. Whether it is preaching, singing, healing, pastoring; the principle is the same. God is in the business of producing many ministers of the same kind.

Learn How to Copy

Decide to become a pastor of a large and growing church. You can have church growth. Decide to be a great man of God; decide to be become the pastor of a huge church. How can you do this?

The answer is simple: copy someone who has done it before you. Do not be mystical about the formula to greatness in God. Do not beat about the bush. Go directly to God's method of producing greatness.

Churches that work are pastored by pastors of a certain kind. Churches that grow are pastored by men and women of a certain kind. Since that is also your vision, why don't you become another of the same kind?

Copying is the way to the anointing. Copying is the key to greatness in God. Copying is the open door for you to enter the things of the kingdom.

If there is a great evangelist, another of the same kind will also be great. If there is an anointed pastor, another of the same kind will also be anointed. If there is a powerful apostle, another of the same kind will be powerful.

You are not special or different. You are simply going to become another of the kind that God has raised up already. You must find someone with a similar calling and follow hard after him.

It won't be long and we will be going home. You don't have much time for trial and error. You cannot afford time for experiments. You may be in the middle of your experiment when the Lord calls you.

You need to get straight to the point. You need the anointing and you need it fast! You need to preach well and you need to preach well now! You need to heal the sick and raise the dead and you need it to happen within the time the Lord has given you.

How many years of experimentation are you going to dabble in until you become humble enough to copy someone's success.

We Are All Copies of Something Else

Begin to accept that we are all copies of something else. I am not some rare species whom Christ has chosen for the end-time move. Such thoughts only lead to error. I am a member of the Lord's army. I stand among the ranks and I am glad to be have been able to copy something that one of my fathers has done.

Do you want to raise up a great church?

Do you want church growth?

Thoughts of being unique will keep you away from learning from obvious examples in front of them. God wants to raise up more mega church pastors.

Is Copying Biblical?

And the earth brought forth grass, and herb yielding seed after his kind...and God saw that it was good. And God created...every living creature ...after their KIND...and God saw that it was good. And God made the beast of the earth after his kind...and God saw that it was good.

Genesis 1:12, 21, 25

Almighty God created things to produce after their kind. The grass produces another of the same kind, the herbs produce another of the same kind, and the whales produce another of the same kind. Even man produces another of the same kind. The Lord God saw that another of the same kind was a good thing! Instead of being preoccupied with producing another of a different kind, let us produce fruit that is a good copy.

And God said, Let us make man in our image, after our likeness...

Genesis 1:26

When the Lord created man, he created something that was like Himself. He said that let us make something that is like us: another of the same kind, a copy. There are many similarities between man and God because we are made in His image. God is a Spirit and the Father of spirits.

Human beings are also spirits living in bodies. God the Father, God the Son and God the Holy Spirit make up the Trinity we know.

Man as spirit, soul and body also makes up a triune being. When men walk in their creative and inventive elements they are clearly copying God.

Chapter 33

Why Copying Will Help
Your Ministry

Copying is the highest and fastest kind of learning.

1. Copying is a God-given method of learning for children.

Children use this method of learning effortlessly and that is why they learn anything easily. This is why children learn languages quickly. Many new things are a struggle for grown-ups to assimilate. Young people have no problems learning new things because they have no inhibitions when it comes to copying.

One day, I heard someone describe some people in his church as "BBTs". Then he said, "I myself am a "BBT".

So I asked him, "What is a BBT"? Who is a "BBT"?

He answered, "A "BBT" is somebody who was "Born Before Technology".

He continued, "Such people cannot learn or use computers and other modern technology."

He explained, "When you have BBTs in charge of certain things the church is not able to move forward."

I thought to myself, "What makes someone a "BBT" is his inability to learn anything using the fastest method of learning – copying! He cannot understand the computers, the software and the other modern gadgets because he does not copy easily."

2. Copying is God's way of making you humble.

...that they without us should not be made perfect.
Hebrews 11:40

181

The world's system teaches that the way to be qualified is to go to school. But the biblical way to becoming anything in the ministry is copying and following. Copying is the natural way by which God reproduces ministers. Pride and presumption will keep us from becoming highly anointed servants.

Think about it; if you were able to do as much as certain people, it would be a great achievement. Forget about outshining others! If you can just be as good as some of the guys ahead of you, you would have achieved a lot.

The ministry is difficult. It takes a lot of grace to even please God.

And I will pray the Father, and he shall give you another Comforter, that he may abide with you for ever;
John 14:16

The Holy Spirit (Comforter) is the anointing. When Jesus promised another comforter of the same kind, He was promising another anointing of the same kind. He was showing that the same kind of anointing with which He had ministered would be available to the apostles when He left.

Most pastors would hasten their progress in the ministry if they would understand this simple truth. There is no new and special anointing that God wants to give you. He is simply going to give you another anointing of the same kind. Even the apostles were promised another of the same kind.

It takes humility to admit that you are not an original. When people are impressed with your ministry, it is not easy to reveal that your message is not original. When people are impressed with your style it is not easy to reveal that you learnt it from somewhere else.

Copying makes you dependent and sheep-like. The sheep nature is different from the serpent nature. It is the nature of snakes to be independent and solitary. This is the very opposite of how you must be if you want to walk with the Lord.

To be another of the same kind, you will have to depend on someone, you will have to learn from someone and you will have to follow someone. It is a good thing because no one can boast except in the Lord who created all things.

Because you are humble, the blessings of God are going to be passed on to another generation.

Not only will there be one great man of God for this generation, but there will be another of the same kind for the next generation.

3. **Copying causes you to discover that there is nothing new under the sun.**

    The thing that hath been, it is that which shall be; and that which is done is that which shall be done: and there is no new thing under the sun. Is there any thing whereof it may be said, See, this is new? it hath been already of old time, which was before us.
    Ecclesiastes 1:9-10

Indeed, there is nothing new under the sun. This is a fact that you must accept. You have nothing new to offer and your life will not introduce anything special.

Like most ministers, I once thought I was introducing something new. I thought I had some new gifts and ideas, which no one else had ever had.

With time, I discovered that all that I was doing had been done before. Every single thing I am doing and saying I have found people who said them before I did.

The truth about my ministry is that I am simply following hard after others I genuinely admire. I want to be like them and I am not ashamed to say so! I like their spirit! I like their flow! If I can be a copy of something that is working it would be a great achievement for me.

4. Copying is good because you become something that is already successful and working.

Copying sets you free from experimentation. You are free from years of wasting time as you discover principles that have worked over and over again.

You do not have to create a new name. Making a name is not easy. That is why names are sold as franchises. A good name is one of the most valuable things on earth. Becoming another of the same kind means you are another with the same kind of name. Copying gives you access to strategies and formulae that have worked for your kind.

When I decide to become another of the same kind, all I need to know are the methods which were used by the one I am copying from. What worked for him will work for me. I simply copy the systems and techniques that have produced the results in him. Since I am going to be another of the same kind, the same kind of methods that worked for him will surely work for me!

5. Copying makes things easier for you on this road of ministry.

Many who are called to the ministry do not know how to walk the road of ministry. They know God has called them but don't have a clue as to how to progress. Many men of God do not know how to climb into higher heights in ministry. They see other men of God accomplishing great things but don't know that they can do the same!

The road to accomplishing the same things is clear now. Humble yourself and become another of the same kind.

Don't try to be unique, special or different. Just become a copy of something that is working. Become another of the same kind. Use the techniques they used. Follow them very closely. Preach what they preach. Pray in the same way that they pray. Seek God in the same way that they do. Have as close a relationship to God as they do. You will surely become a marvelous copy of something successful.

6. Copying helps you to enter new things faster.

Copying quickens your rate of advancement in life and ministry. Because you are following a well-chartered road, you have the benefit of those who went on before you. The things that slowed them will not slow you down. You will move through obstacles faster because your kind will give you tips on how to overcome.

Without experiments and trials, anyone would be faster. One day, I was going somewhere with someone. He was in his car ahead and I was in mine. When he got into traffic, he called me and told me not to come the way he had gone because there was too much traffic on his route. I ended up getting there faster than he did because he saved me from having to go through his problem.

7. Copying helps to overcome problems.

Problems of a particular kind usually have the same solution. When you copy someone you will learn from the solutions he has developed. His experience at tackling the same problems will be yours.

Have you ever wondered why doctors are calm in the face of apparent emergencies? It is because they are following solutions that have been repeated over and over for the same kind of problem.

8. Copying is the natural way to increase.

The natural way that all of creation multiplies is by producing another of the same kind. .

And the earth brought forth grass, and herb yielding seed after his kind ...and God saw that it was good. And God created ...every living CREATURE ...after their KIND ...and God saw that it was good. And God made the beast of the earth after his kind ...and God saw that it was good.

Genesis 1:12, 21, 25

The natural way that the church will grow from glory to glory is to shamelessly learn from those ahead. I do not dispute that there are other ways to move forward. But I can share what has worked for me. *Copy! Copy! Copy!* Become another of the same kind. I want to be like my fathers who have gone ahead of me. I want to be exactly like them. I want to be like Jesus. I don't need to have any unique characteristics.

9. Copying is the key to great teaching and preaching.

Hear another parable: There was a certain householder, which planted a vineyard, and hedged it round about, and digged a winepress in it, and built a tower, and let it out to husbandmen, and went into a far country:
Matthew 21:33

Jesus taught the Word of God in the most beautiful and anointed way ever known to man. Little children remember his stories long after they stop reading the Bible. His teachings are relevant two thousand years after He gave them.

The things that Jesus said are read by more people, quoted by more authors, translated into more languages, set to more music and represented in more art than any book ever written by man.

As someone said, comparing the teachings of Socrates, Plato and Aristotle to those of Jesus is like comparing an enquiry with a revelation!

Years ago, I told my beloved that I wanted to be a teacher of the Word like Jesus was. I thought to myself, "The teachings of Jesus are not easily forgotten, even by children." I decided to copy Jesus. Years ago, before I became a pastor, I decided to teach and preach with stories.

Jesus told so many stories. He would say, "A certain man had two sons..., a certain man made a great party..., there was a certain rich man which was clothed in purple..., a certain rich man died..., a certain man went up from Jericho..., there was a certain rich man which had a steward..., the ground of a certain rich man brought forth bountifully…, a certain noble man went into a far country…"

I decided that I wanted to be a teacher like Jesus. I didn't want to be anything new; I just wanted to be an exact copy of Jesus Christ.

The key to becoming a great preacher is to copy another great preacher. Just find a preacher whose ministry touches lives and become another of the same kind. Learn how to preach by copying! Don't blame anyone for your dry preaching. Don't blame anyone if no one listens to you! You know what to do.

Preach in the same way, teach in the same way and you will be very successful. Don't try anything new because there is nothing new.

I don't know how plainer I could be when I say you should "copy"? Shamelessly copy, photocopy, photograph, replay, rewind and repeat what those great men do. You will find yourself becoming another of the same kind!

Those who are too proud to do this deliberately are becoming copies of somebody anyway. Why not choose and become a copy of somebody you admire? Why not choose to be a copy of someone whom God has sent into your life to train and mentor you?

Section 14

CHURCH GROWTH AND
HARD WORK

Chapter 34

Church Growth and the Constant Effort to Accomplish

Diligence

Church growth is accomplished through constant effort. Without persistence in seeking the growth of the church, you will never have a mega church. Many pastors are unwilling to apply the relentless, unremitting and exacting efforts that are required to accomplish church growth. The church, like a farm, will require you to bestow much labour on it.

Diligence is the constant and earnest effort to accomplish what is undertaken. Diligence is the persistent exertion of your body and mind towards your goal. People just want hands to be laid on them so that they can receive the magical gift of a mega church. But church growth does not happen that way. Church growth happens by being attentive and persistent in building the church. Church growth happens through diligence.

Church growth will be given to pastors who believe in diligence. Church growth will be given to pastors who are relentless in their pursuit of church expansion.

Seven Rewards for Your Constant Efforts

1. **Pastors who exert a constant effort to accomplish church growth can expect to be found without spot and blameless.**

   Wherefore, beloved, seeing that ye look for such things, be DILIGENT that ye may be found of him in peace, WITHOUT SPOT, AND BLAMELESS.

   2 Peter 3:14

2. **Pastors who exert a constant effort to accomplish church growth can expect to become rich through their work.**

He becometh poor that dealeth with a slack hand: but the hand of the DILIGENT MAKETH RICH.

Proverbs 10:4

3. **Pastors who exert a constant effort to accomplish church growth can expect to become men of authority in charge of huge churches.**

The hand of the DILIGENT shall BEAR RULE: but the slothful shall be under tribute.

Proverbs 12:24

4. **Pastors who exert a constant effort to accomplish church growth can expect to be made anointed, prosperous and fat.**

The soul of the sluggard desireth, and hath nothing: but the soul of the DILIGENT shall BE MADE FAT.

Proverbs 13:4

5. **Pastors who exert a constant effort to accomplish church growth can expect plenteousness in church members and church growth.**

The thoughts of the DILIGENT tend only to plenteousness; but of every one that is hasty only to want.

Proverbs 21:5

6. **Pastors who exert a constant effort to accomplish church growth can expect to gain access to the corridors of power and influence.**

Seest thou a man DILIGENT in his business? he shall STAND BEFORE KINGS; he shall not stand before mean men.

Proverbs 22:29

7. **Pastors who exert a constant effort to accomplish church growth can expect to have a great ministry that will last many generations.**

Be thou DILIGENT to know the state of thy flocks, and look well to thy herds. For riches are not for ever: and doth the crown endure to EVERY GENERATION?

Proverbs 27:23-24

Chapter 35

How to Work Hard for a Mega Church

Let the elders who rule well be considered worthy of double honor, especially THOSE WHO WORK HARD at preaching and teaching.

1 Timothy 5:17 (NASB)

How do you become an industrious worker, occupied all the time with the Lord's work?

How do you become an effective, tenacious and tireless minister of the gospel? How can you be relentless in your drive for church growth? This chapter seeks to show you how to work hard as a pastor.

1. Work hard by using the most fruitful working hours.

Every true job has its own working hours. The work of the ministry has its own peculiar working hours. This often confuses people. They think pastors must be in the office from 9:00 a.m. to 5:00 p.m. like everybody else.

But those are the fruitful working hours of secular offices. But we are not bankers or accountants. We are ministers of the gospel!

No more banking hours for pastors! Nobody asks pilots to work from 9:00 a.m. to 5:00 p.m. Everybody knows that their working hours are peculiar and everyone accepts that reality.

Helps ministers and church administrators may have to work from 8.00am to 5.00pm like secular workers because of the nature of their ministry work. But shepherding pastors will have completely different fruitful working hours.

On Sunday mornings, our church boots into action at 6.00am and we sometimes leave after midnight. Sunday is the church's busiest and most important day for the pastor. A Sunday well spent is like a whole week of work! It should be the case for every church. Pastors counsel, visit, and teach Bible school classes throughout the whole of Sunday. Pastors who are building their churches must rest on Mondays.

2. Work hard by spending a lot of time on the church.

When an activity consumes just a few minutes of your time in a week, it cannot be called your "work". For instance, I drive my car for a few minutes every day but my work is not "driving" per se. It is something that I do on my way to work.

However, if driving a car, for example a taxi, were to become my work, I would not spend less than eight hours a day driving. Then, to me, driving would have become work!

You cannot claim to be doing the "work" of the ministry until it actually consumes a reasonable amount of time in your week.

If waiting on God, catching the anointing, catching revelation and receiving guidance from the Holy Spirit does not take up many hours and days of your week, then you are not working yet. For a minister of the gospel, praying and waiting on God must take up many hours. If it is work it will take up your time.

When you were not a pastor building a large church, you could afford to spend a few minutes catching the anointing. You could afford to spend twenty minutes receiving a revelation from the Word. But now that you are a serious professional mega church builder, you need to spend several hours and days waiting on the Lord!

3. Work hard by expending your energy and money on the church.

Everyone must realize that doing the work of the ministry involves spending a lot of energy. Do not be surprised if you get tired doing the work of a pastor. It is only a sign that you are working well. Most good jobs leave their employees exhausted. Do not be surprised if the ministry leaves you tired and worn out.

Another thing that you will expend is money. Does it not cost you money to go to work everyday? Do you not spend money at work for lunch everyday?

It is the same thing with the work of ministry. Why should you complain if you have to pay money to travel to wait on the Lord? Why should you complain if you have to spend money buying books and CDs that you need?

Make no mistake about it. Waiting on God, catching the anointing and revelation by the guidance of the Spirit is hard work. Praying, visiting, counseling and interacting with people is hard work.

As you do the work of God, you will expend your energy and money. When you begin to feel tired, just remember it is a sign that you are really working.

4. Work hard by cheerfully doing the same things over and over.

By nature, all real work is repetitive and regular. If you are working hard you will do the repetitive and regular chores cheerfully. Even if you are bored you must keep doing the "work" - praying, visiting, counseling and interacting (PVCI). Even if you are tired you must keep doing the "work" – waiting on God, catching the anointing, catching the revelation and guidance (WAR).

Many pastors don't pray much because they feel it's repetitive and boring. But when prayer becomes your work you will have to repeat your prayers and you will have to pray regularly. When visiting becomes your work, you will have to visit repeatedly and regularly.

There is a difference between a social visit to a friend's house and a pastoral visit. Pastoral visits must be conducted repeatedly by pastors. Mega church pastors must intentionally go to the homes of their members on a regular basis.

Don't we do our secular work when we don't feel like it? Don't we all go to the same work place repeatedly and regularly although we don't feel like it?

In the same way, anyone who claims to be doing the work of the ministry must rise up and repeatedly do the important tasks of a pastor. We don't pray just because we feel like it. We pray because we have to! We must rise up early and cheerfully intercede for the people God has given us.

5. Work hard under an overseer.

To Titus, my true child in a common faith: ...For this reason I left you in Crete, that you might set in order what remains, and appoint elders in every city AS I DIRECTED YOU,

Titus 1:4-5 (NASB)

Paul directed Timothy and Titus in the ministry. He told them what to do, where to stay and even what to say.

He sent them on errands and missions in the ministry.

Timothy and Titus are good examples of ministers who worked under the oversight of an apostle.

They received detailed instructions on how to behave in the church. The reality is that most ministers need to be supervised.

Unfortunately, some people develop an attitude when they are supervised. They frown and sulk when they are instructed or corrected. They threaten to break away when they are told off. They say, "The church structure is too rigid, too tight and too inflexible. We need space to operate and develop our ministries."

Because supervised people are paid less than the unsupervised they often break away because of money. Working diligently under an overseer will only lead to your promotion.

6. Work hard when you have no overseer.

For I would have you know, brethren, that the gospel which was preached by me is not according to man.

> **For I neither received it from man, nor was I taught it,
> but I received it through a revelation of Jesus Christ.**
>
> **Galatians 1:11-12 (NASB)**

Paul is the best example of a minister who had no overseer. He did not need to be supervised. No one told him where to go or what to say. Your calling may be such that you do not need an overseer.

When you have no overseer, you need maturity in hearing the voice of the Holy Spirit. You need accuracy in hearing the voice of the Holy Spirit. You need to be able to judge yourself since there is no one around to judge you.

Nobody will tell you are wrong. No one will tell you when to pray, study or visit anyone. God will have to tell you directly.

When you are not supervised, no one will speak to you about the changes you have to make in your ministry or the decisions you have to take.

No one will tell you when you are going astray or when you are moving into error. You have to judge yourself. And your judgment had better be right. If you have not been called into this kind of unsupervised position do not venture into it because it will destroy you. Many ministers have become independent and self-governing when they should have lived and ministered under the supervision of a true apostle like Paul.

7. Work hard by working from your heart.

> **For I have no man likeminded, who will naturally care
> for your state.**
>
> **Philippians 2:20**

There is nothing like doing a job from the bottom of your heart. Work for God until it becomes your second nature. Work for the Lord until it is a pleasure for you to work. Work for the Lord until you cannot distinguish between working and resting.

No one ever told me what to do in ministry. I have naturally wanted to pray, to visit and to counsel my people. I have naturally wanted to wait on God, catch the anointing, revelation and receive guidance from the Holy Spirit.

Our church is larger today and I struggle to know the names of everyone and to remember who they are. It is almost an impossible task! I wish I knew everybody's homes. I wish I could attend all their important family events. It is a natural desire. Anyone who is a true pastor has what I call "natural care".

Chapter 36

Church Growth and the Work of a Pastor (P.V.C.I.)

... LET HIM LABOUR, working with his hands the thing which is good...

Ephesians 4:28

I remember when I first started out in full-time ministry. People would often ask my wife, "Where is your husband? Is he at home?"

One lady, a lawyer friend of hers said, "Oh, so your husband doesn't work anymore!"

My wife would answer, "You have no idea how hard he works."

They thought that because I was no longer practicing medicine, I was no longer working. Many people think that all that the pastor does is to prepare one sermon a week and then deliver it on Sunday morning. Afterwards, he is free to sleep until the next Sunday.

Many times people have called either late in the morning or in the afternoon and have said, "Hullo, how are you pastor? Sorry to disturb your sleep."

I would think, "This man thinks I sleep all day and all night as well."

Then I would politely answer, "I was not sleeping."

I have never bothered to explain what I was doing. "It is a waste of time," I thought to myself.

These and other remarks have made me realize that some people think that the ministry is a very restful occupation—an easy alternative to real and difficult jobs.

Three Reasons Why Ministry Is Hard Work!

1. Ministry is hard work because Paul taught that ministry was work.

And he gave some, apostles; and some, prophets; and some, evangelists; and some, pastors and teachers; For the perfecting of the saints, for the WORK of the ministry, for the edifying of the body of Christ:

Ephesians 4:11-12

The saints are to be perfected for the work. This means that pastors are to perfect the saints so that *they* can join in the hard work of ministry.

2. Ministry is hard work because Epaphras laboured in ministry work.

Epaphras, who is *one* of you, a servant of Christ, saluteth you, always labouring fervently for you in prayers, that ye may stand perfect and complete in all the will of God.

Colossians 4:12

There was a man called Epaphras, a servant of Christ "always labouring fervently for you in prayers". Epaphras was not playing games. He was not on a holiday. He was labouring, working and fighting for the kingdom of God.

3. Ministry is hard work because Jesus described the workers in ministry as labourers.

When Jesus saw the multitudes who were fainting because of lack of a shepherd, He said, "The harvest is plenty but the labourers are few."

The Greek word translated labourer is the word "ergates", which means a toiler, teacher, laborer and a worker.

The ministry is toil and sweat. I have found that out practically. Anybody who wants to have a mega church must realize that he is not embarking on a game but real work. You

199

will soon realize that church growth is not a joke and neither is it a game. It is real toil and labour. If ministry is work, what does it involve? What type of work is ministry work?

The Pastor's Work: PVCI

PRAYER (P) VISITATION (V) COUNSELLING (C) INTERACTION (I)

1. PRAYER

Prayer is the sustaining force of the church. I believe in praying for hours for the church. There is a correlation between the amount of prayer put into the church by the eldership of the church and the growth of the church.

In Korea, it is well known that the pastors pray for long hours. It is no surprise then that the largest churches in the world are found in that nation.

I believe that every full-time pastor should try to pray for at least three hours every day. Lay pastors and shepherds should pray for at least one or two hours a day. There must be long times of prayer.

2. VISITATION

In Jeremiah 23:2, God makes it clear that one of the principal duties of pastors is to visit.

> **Therefore thus saith the Lord God of Israel against the pastors...Ye have scattered my flock...and HAVE NOT VISITED THEM...**
>
> **Jeremiah 23:2**

It is quite clear from this, that pastors are expected to visit their sheep in their homes. This is different from counseling them in the office. It is also different from preaching and teaching from the pulpit. It is a special ministry. The greatest visitor on this earth was Jesus Christ. Since his visit, the world has never been the same again.

There is a difference between church members who have been visited and those who have never been visited. Church members who have been visited in their homes become stable and hardly ever leave the church.

3. COUNSELLING

It is important to minister the Word of God, especially in teaching. Churches based on solid Bible teachings tend to grow. As the years go by, these churches grow larger and larger. It is like a flock that has been exposed to fields and fields of green grass. The natural response is that the flock will be healthy, multiply and grow.

You will find greater growth in churches that have strong teaching and preaching than in churches that emphasize miracles.

I believe in miracles but these can never take the place of the Word. Sheep don't feed on miracles. They feed on the Word!

4. INTERACTION

A shepherd is supposed to interact with his sheep. How can he interact properly if he is detached and aloof? Pastors and shepherds must do what I call *"Deep Sea Fishing"*.

Deep Sea Fishing

What is the deep sea? The deep sea is the mass of church members who stream in and out of church every Sunday morning. Many people attend our churches and nobody knows them or even talks with them. Some come in and out for a while and then drop out.

It is the duty of shepherds and pastors to plunge into what I call the deep sea and conduct *Deep Sea Fishing.* They are to move into the crowd of unknown faces and interact with them. They must befriend unknown people, talk with them, find out where they live, and establish a line of friendship.

Everybody wants to be known and to feel important. When people are not known, they move away to a place where they can be known and made to feel important. All human beings have a psychological need to be identified and recognized!

It is that need that we try to meet by doing *"deep sea fishing"*.

When all the pastors do deep sea fishing, they will get to know the people who do not belong to small groups within the church, but still need pastoral visits and care.

Deep sea fishing helps to establish floating visitors in the church.

That is why it is important for lay pastors and shepherds to be in church on Sunday and involve themselves in this all-important interaction - *deep sea fishing*. It is not only the pastor who is preaching who has work to do.

I like to linger in the church for hours after the service, interacting with different people and meeting different groups.

I am neither a Prime Minister nor a pop star. I am a pastor. Pastors are not film stars. They are shepherds who are supposed to mingle with their sheep. The Bible says that the sheep know the voice of the good shepherd. How can they know your voice if they don't even see you?

Chapter 37

Church Growth and the Work of Taking Heed to Yourself (W.A.R.)

Take heed unto thyself, and unto the doctrine; continue in them: for in doing this thou shalt both save thyself, and them that hear thee.

1 Timothy 4:16

Take heed to yourself so that you can become a mega church pastor. The ministry depends on you because you are the shepherd. If you go down everything will go down with you. You must invest in yourself. You must protect yourself and you must help yourself.

The work of taking heed to yourself involves four main things just as the work of pastoring a church involves four main things. The four main things we need to do to take heed to yourself are: Waiting on God, catching the Anointing, catching revelation and receiving guidance from the Holy Spirit (W.A.R.)

The Work of Saving Yourself: WAR

WAITING (W) ANOINTING (A) REVELATION (R)

1. WAITING

We must wait on the Lord! Learn our lessons well. In His timing He will tell where to go, what to do and what to say. Pastors and shepherds should make it a point to get away from their busy schedules and wait on God for even longer periods. Jesus himself retreated to the wilderness and mountains to pray. Praying for whole days on retreats is a very important aspect of a pastor's schedule.

203

Waiting actually involves pausing, slowing down and not rushing headlong into things.

The ministry is spiritual from beginning to end.

Full-time ministry always involves prayer and ministry of the Word.

...It is not reason that we should leave the word of God, and serve tables... But we will give ourselves continually to prayer, and to the ministry of the word.

Acts 6:2-4

Peter made it clear that his work was not arranging tables nor organizing food for his church members. His duty was to pray and minister the Word.

2. ANOINTING

How God anointed Jesus of Nazareth with the Holy Ghost and with power: who went about doing good, and healing all that were oppressed of the devil; for God was with him.

Acts 10:38

You will receive several anointings in the course of your life. Different gifts will be imparted to you at different times. These different gifts are given to you at different times depending on what you are doing in the ministry. You cannot go around doing the good work of building large churches unless you are anointed to do so.

The anointing is the Holy Spirit and Jesus taught us to pray for the Holy Spirit. You must spend hours and hours praying for the Holy Spirit. God will give you what you ask for.

Apart from receiving the Holy Spirit on the day of Pentecost, (Acts 2:4) several other impartations of the gifts of the Holy Spirit took place.

Jesus breathed on the disciples at a meeting and asked them to receive the Holy Spirit (John 20:22).

On another occasion when the disciples were assembled they were filled again with the Holy Spirit and empowered for miracles, signs and wonders (Acts 4:31).

3. REVELATION

That the God of our Lord Jesus Christ, the Father of glory, may give unto you the spirit of wisdom and revelation in the knowledge of him
Ephesians 1:17

Revelation for Preaching

Revelation is an instance of communication and disclosure that God gives to His servants. God discloses His word and His will to those that He loves.

Have you ever thought about it? Revelation is the one thing that sets you above your congregation and enables you to lead them.

Think about it. If God has revealed something to you that He did not reveal to others, He must regard you differently. Revelation is what sets you apart from the ordinary Christian.

Kenneth Hagin shared how he had prayed for the spirit of wisdom and revelation for years and years on end. It also became my prayer as I sought after the Lord.

Study to shew thyself approved unto God, a workman that needeth not to be ashamed, rightly dividing the word of truth.
2 Timothy 2:15

Receiving revelation is key to the success of your ministry. Revelation has several parts to it. Revelation can be from the word of God or from visions and dreams. A pastor must spend his time seeking revelation from God. The spirit of revelation is evident when a person preaches or teaches the Word of God.

Revelation from the Word of God is the most beautiful kind of revelation and you must spend time seeking for it. "No man ever spake like this man," is what they will say when the Spirit of revelation is upon you.

Ten Ways to Receive Revelation

1. You receive revelation when you listen to anointed messages from preachers and teachers of the Word of God. (Ephesians 4:11-12).

2. You receive revelation when you study the Word of God in relation to sermons and messages you have recently heard. (2 Timothy 2:15).

3. You receive revelation when you study the Word of God and search for the deeper meanings of words in the Bible. (2 Peter 1:21).

4. You receive revelation when you have discussions with fellow pastors, teachers and prophets. (Acts 13:1-3).

5. You receive revelation when you read the real life stories of men of God that have gone ahead of you. (Acts 1:1).

6. You receive revelation when you study the dreams and visions of well-recognized prophets. I have received much revelation for my life by studying the visions and dreams of Kenneth Hagin and Rick Joyner. (John 20:17-18).

7. You receive revelation when God reminds you of something important. Don't take it lightly when you suddenly remember something you have forgotten. (John 14:26).

8. You receive revelation when the Lord puts a burden on your heart. (Jeremiah 23:32-40).

9. You receive revelation when God impresses something on your heart through the inner witness. (Romans 8:16).

10. You receive revelation when God speaks to you through a dream or a vision. (Acts 16:9).

Revelation for Guidance

For as many as are led by the Spirit of God, they are the sons of God.

Romans 8:14

One of the key aspects of revelation is the guidance that it brings. You must be led by the Holy Spirit in all that you do for God. Every detail matters to God. He wants to know and He wants to direct. You cannot just have a radio programme because everyone is doing it.

When you are led by the Spirit of God, you become a son of God. A son of God is a supernatural being who operates under the powers granted by his heavenly father.

Being led by the spirit of God makes you have a supernatural ministry. It is supernatural to have thousands of people gathering every Sunday to listen to your wisdom.

Kenneth Hagin said the difference between ministers is their ability to be led by the Spirit of God.

One of the key duties of a minister is to wait and seek for supernatural guidance concerning everything that he is doing. Waiting on God for supernatural guidance is no small task. It is a big job and will take up hours, days and weeks of searching for the will of God.

Two Missing Ingredients

There are two things that are often missing in a minister's life: the manifestations of God and the presence of God. Supernatural guidance and obedience to God's will are the keys to the manifestations and the presence of the Lord. You must relate with ministers not just by their good doctrines. You must relate with them because you sense the presence of God in their lives.

Why should you bother to get close to ministries that have no spiritual glory on them; from whence the glory of the Lord has departed? Why do you have something to do with someone whom God is not with?

How to Minister with the Manifestation of God

The key to the manifestations of God is obedience to His Word. Whether this Word came through the reading of the Bible or through a dream, you must obey it. It is the only thing you can do to show Him that you love Him. God will manifest Himself to you when you obey His instructions. Read for yourself the promise of the manifestations of God:

> **He that hath my commandments, and keepeth them, he it is that loveth me: and he that loveth me shall be loved of my Father, and I will love him, and will MANIFEST myself to him.**
>
> **John 14:21**

How to Minister with the Presence of God

You must seek to obey the will of God when He shows it to you. It is the key to the presence of the Lord. The presence of God will come on you because you are obeying the words and instructions to your life. Read for yourself the promise of the presence of God:

> **Jesus answered and said unto him, If a man love me, he will keep my words: and my Father will love him, and we will come unto him, and make our abode with him.**
>
> **John 14:23**

Section 15

CHURCH GROWTH AND OUTWARD IMPRESSIONS

Chapter 38

Church Growth and
Outward Impressions

... that ye may have somewhat to answer them which glory in appearance, and not in heart.

2 Corinthians 5:12

The Bible teaches us to have something to answer those who glory in outward appearances. There are always people who live and take decisions purely by the outward appearance. Most of the people in our churches are carnal people. Carnal people usually judge by outward appearances because they are not spiritual.

Whether you like it or not outward appearances matter in church growth. To have a mega church, you must be able to relate with and impress many carnal people who judge by outward appearances.

Once you are dealing with men you will be dealing with outward appearances. Indeed, the Lord does not look at these appearances but men do. "... for the LORD seeth not as man seeth; for man looketh on the outward appearance, but the Lord looketh on the heart" (1 Samuel 16:7).

If man looks on the outward appearance then you need to get your outward appearances in order.

Ten Areas Where Outward Impressions Are Important

1. **The outward appearance of your church building will affect your church growth.**

Is your church housed in a ramshackle and decrepit building? Is your church building painted? Is it neat? Is there rubbish everywhere? Is there a refreshing and well-designed sign directing people to the service? Is your church building hot, stuffy and airless?

2. The outward appearance of the location of your church building will affect your church growth.

Is your church located in a disreputable or dangerous place? Are people afraid to come to that area? The location of your church will definitely affect the people who come there.

3. The outward appearance of your stage will affect your church growth.

Is your stage well lit and well organized? Or is it overcrowded? Are the instruments properly arranged and positioned on the stage?

Is there symmetry on the stage? Is the stage simply a collection of odd items, many of which are not used during the church service?

What is the character of your decorations? Does your stage have an international feel to it? Or have you allowed someone with poor taste to decorate your stage according to the low standards that she knows?

4. The outward appearance of the pastor will affect your church growth.

Do you dress nicely? Is your suit two sizes bigger than you are? Have you ironed your clothes until they are stiff and shiny phantoms of the original? Are your shoes dusty? Is your shirt falling off your shoulders? Are your teeth yellow?

Do you have missing teeth that make you look like Dracula when you smile? Are any of your teeth sticking out or pointing in the wrong direction that make you look like a predator when you speak to the congregants?

You may need to get a dentist to correct all that. You will be surprised at how improving the appearance of your teeth can lead to church growth.

5. The outward appearance of the pastor's wife will affect church growth.

Does the pastor's wife have a nice hairstyle? Or is her hair simply a black oily rag that has been dumped on her head?

Does she bother to make herself beautiful? Does she have nice dresses and shoes? Does she smile? Is she friendly? Is she hospitable? Or is she ill-natured and quarrelsome? Does she look like a witch?

Does she have a grim and unfriendly look? Does she constantly fall into depression and black moods?

The negative outward characteristics of a pastor's wife will definitely affect church growth.

6. The outward appearance of the pastor's children will affect church growth.

Barefooted, scruffy little ragamuffins running all over the place will not help your church grow. If the pastor's children are constantly wear ill-fitting and dirty clothes, it will not improve the outward image of your church. A thriving prosperous church does not have little children who look like beggars or beggars' children running all over the place.

7. The outward appearance of the associate pastors will affect your church growth.

Do your associate pastors look like a group of nobodies? Are they significant leaders in the congregation? Do they dress well? Do your associate pastors act like wimps constantly exuding timidity and false humility? Do they constantly have sheepish smiles? Are they constantly trying to please the richer members of the congregation?

Do your assistant pastors have cars? Are they happy people who breed confidence, loyalty and unity?

8. **The outward appearance of the pastor's car will affect your church growth.**

Is your car the oldest model of its type? Is it always breaking down; making you have to beg for lifts and favours? This will not help church growth.

Is your car the most expensive car in the church? Why do you want to look like the richest member of your church? Are you a business tycoon or a pastor?

Why don't you rather blend into the congregation and be seen as an average person, neither the richest nor the poorest?

9. **The outward appearance of the ushers will affect your church growth.**

Do your ushers look like lean hungry foxes ready to steal offerings from the basket? Or do they look like dignified gentlemen who are humble servants in the house of the Lord? Do they know how to walk and carry themselves?

10. **The outward appearance of the choristers and musicians will affect your church growth.**

Do your choristers and musicians look nice? Do they do their hair and wear nice clothes?

Are they so clumsy that they cannot fit into their clothes nor walk up the stage?

Do they have nice voices or do they shriek through the microphone every Sunday?

Are they smiling, happy worshippers of the Lord?

Section 16

CHURCH GROWTH AND WOMEN

Chapter 39

Seven Reasons Why Women Make a Church Grow

Women are one of the greatest assets a church could ever have. Satan has deployed his weapon of deception to keep the women out of the workforce. Women have been depicted as the most dangerous group of people ready to destroy the man of God and his ministry. Indeed, many strange women have done just that!

However, this same group of apparently dangerous people hold the key to church growth. Women believe more quickly and are more ready to flow with God's servant. When churches are being pioneered, women are often the greatest treasure the apostle could have.

1. **Women will make your church grow because they helped Jesus in His ministry. In the Bible women followed Jesus and helped Him.**

If women helped Jesus I would like them to help me too. If Jesus needed the help of women, you will too.   Jesus had a worldwide ministry. He travelled to many cities and villages preaching the gospel. The twelve disciples were with Him on these preaching tours as well as certain women who ministered to Him. Women are always present where fruits are being borne!

> And it came about soon afterwards, that He began going about from one city and village to another, proclaiming and preaching the kingdom of God; and THE TWELVE WERE WITH HIM, AND ALSO SOME WOMEN who had been healed of evil spirits and sicknesses: Mary who was called Magdalene, from whom seven demons had gone out, and Joanna the wife of Chuza, Herod's steward, and Susanna, and many others who were contributing to their support out of their private means.
>
> Luke 8:1- 3 (NASB)

2. Women will make your church grow because the apostle Paul used women in his ministry.

If women helped the apostle Paul to achieve so much for God, they must have some importance other than making meat pies, serving tea or frying fish! Women can be fellow labourers with apostles in the ministry.

> And I intreat thee also, true yokefellow, help THOSE WOMEN WHICH LABOURED WITH ME in the gospel, with Clement also, and *with* other my fellowlabourers, whose names are in the book of life.
>
> Philippians 4:3

3. Women will make your church grow because they recognize the anointing and believe in it quicker than men.

Indeed, women are the live wires of the anointing. They receive, they detect and they believe ten times faster than the average man.

Abigail recognized that David was going to become the king and she honoured him whilst her husband was hardened and resistant.

The woman with the issue of blood received the anointing whilst Peter, James and the others felt and received no healing anointing at the crusade.

Mary Magdalene went to the graveside on Easter Sunday to experience the resurrection first hand whilst Peter, James, John and the other powerful apostles were huddled away in unbelief and depression.

You may have heard of the Azusa street revival whose leader was William Seymour. There was a man called Charles Parham who was William Seymour's spiritual father and the principal of the Bible School William Seymour attended.

Pentecostalism was born when Charles Parham taught his Bible students (including William Seymour) about receiving the

Holy Spirit and speaking in tongues in his Bible school although he himself did not yet speak in tongues.

Agnes

A lady called Agnes pressurized Charles Parham to pray for her to receive this Holy Spirit.

Charles Parham was reluctant to pray for her but she pressed him to. When Charles Parham prayed for her, a glow came over her and she received the Holy Spirit and began to speak in fluent Chinese tongues. She even received the ability to write in Chinese. This was apparently documented by the government.

Amazingly, the Azusa street revival and the worldwide Pentecostal movement began through this lady being the first to believe and receive this gift of speaking in tongues.

It was after this that William Seymour moved to California and began what we know as the Azusa Street Revival. Indeed, William Seymour himself had not yet received the Holy Spirit when he moved to California.

4. Women will make your church grow because God has destined to destroy the devil through women.

Women will destroy the devil. The ancient prophecy that attests to this fact is that women will bruise the head of the serpent. Through women you will destroy the devil, that old serpent that deceived the world.

> And I will put enmity between thee and the woman, and between thy seed and her seed; it shall bruise thy head, and thou shalt bruise his heel.
>
> Genesis 3:15

5. Women will make your church grow because women are the producers of children.

Wherever there are women there are children, off springs and fruits. In the natural, women bring about and nurture young ones. In the ministry, the same pattern is seen. Wherever there are women there are lots of spiritual children. Somehow, women attract other people to the church and convince many to join. They are the first to believe and the first to convince others to join in.

6. Women will make your church grow because women are good pastors.

Women have the natural gift of talking. They have this gift because they are always talking to children as they bring them up. This gift of talking can be perfectly transposed into the ministry as counsel, teaching and interaction.

I have watched as women have cared for others and built large churches. God used Aimee Semple McPherson to build the Four Square denomination of churches which is a thriving ministry today.

7. Women will make a church grow because women they are good helpers.

Women are natural helpers because they were created by God to help. Every woman has an inbuilt engine that makes her a natural helper. Women are looking for someone to help.

Many women entered their marriages hoping to fulfill their divine calling of helping someone. Unfortunately, the hurts and confusion of marriage do not allow them to use their helping gift. In the church many women are able to express this natural helping gift.

8. Women will make a church grow because they are more permanent and loyal workers.

A church grows proportionately to the number of permanent and loyal people it has. Men are known to change their jobs at least four times in their lives whilst many women keep their jobs for a lifetime. A church filled with faithful and loyal people is a great blessing.

9. **Women will make a church grow because they are less concerned about money than men.**

Women are usually not as interested in money as men. They seem to be more content if they feel safe, secure and happy. Generally speaking, I would prefer to have women counting the church money. Generally speaking, I would prefer to have women in certain sensitive positions.

10. **Women will make a church grow because the largest churches in the world have used women to build their churches.**

Pastor David Yonggi Cho speaks about how women have served faithfully as cell leaders and helped to build his church.

I once preached in a large church that seated twelve thousand people. It was one of the largest churches in that country. In that service, I was amazed to find not more than twenty men amongst twelve thousand women. Amazing women!

Section 17

CHURCH GROWTH RADIO, TELEVISION AND BUSES

Chapter 40

How Radio, Television and Buses Make a Church Grow

... according to the prince of the power of the air...
Ephesians 2:2, KJV

A Vision

A prophet shared a vision. In the vision, he found himself out on the street witnessing. No one was listening to him and he was not getting far with his evangelistic outreach. Then he met an angel who asked him what he was doing. He explained to the angel that he was on outreach doing house-to-house evangelism and door-to-door witnessing.

Then the angel said to him, "Follow me, I will show you another way."

The angel took him to a very long pole stuck in the ground and climbed with him to the very top. The angel said to him, "Call out the people from here and speak to them from this place."

As the pastor sat on the top of the pole and ministered, crowds began to gather and come to him. He was amazed at the response that he was getting by speaking from the top of the pole.

The Lord said to him, "Move away from door to door evangelism and call out to the people through the airwaves. I will bless your ministry as you summon the people through the airwaves."

This vision is a revelation of the importance of radio and television ministry for church growth. The media has an important role to play in our current world. Satan is the prince of the power of the air. He has dominated the airwaves and the church must rise up to take control of the airwaves and dominate it through the gospel of Jesus Christ. The media ministry is a fight against the prince of the power of the air!

Ten Steps to an Effective Radio Ministry

1. BELIEVE IN THE RADIO MINISTRY. Whatever you do that is not of faith is sin. What you do out of faith will work out. Mountains will be moved and rivers will be crossed as you press into the radio ministry. Understand the advantages and blessings of a radio ministry. You must know that you will reach people through the radio whom you will not reach in any other way.

2. BE LED BY THE SPIRIT before you embark on a radio ministry. Pray about the radio ministry and put it before the Lord. If He gives you peace about it then go for it. If it is not his will or his time then stay away from it. If you are led by the Spirit to be on the radio, it will be a blessing to the church. If you are not led by the Spirit to be on radio it will not help you.

3. Have a radio programme EARLY IN THE MORNING in your town or city. Your voice must be heard every morning in your city. Your voice must be heard preaching, praying for people and ministering to all who tune in.

4. Have a radio programme EVERYDAY. For your radio ministry to be effective it must be every day or every weekday.

5. PREPARE for your radio programme as you would for a Sunday sermon. In all labour there is profit and your diligence will cause you to stand before kings. Do not come to the studio unprepared and fumble through the programme.

6. MINISTER TO PEOPLE on the radio as though they are in front of you. Speak as though you were speaking to thousands. Do not wonder to yourself whether people are listening or not. Many people are listening to you.

7. PRAY FOR PEOPLE on the radio. People love to be prayed for. Pray powerful prayers using the King James language, the Psalms and the Synonyms.

8. Never forget to invite PEOPLE to come to your church. Use your time on the radio wisely. Tell people what to do and they will obey you. Invite them to come and see you so that you can continue ministering the power and the anointing to them.

9. DO ALTAR CALLS for salvation and healing. Salvation must never go to the background of your ministry. Jesus Christ came to this world purposely to save sinners. Use the radio to lead people to Jesus Christ. All ministry flourishes on the foundation of Jesus Christ.

10. ASK FOR SUPPORT at the right time. Do not be ashamed to ask for money. Ask and you shall receive, knock and the door shall be opened unto you. The work of a pastor includes asking for support for the ministry.

    But remember that there is a time for everything. Do not start your radio ministry by asking for money. The first thing you do must be to minister the Word of God.

Steps to an Effective TV Ministry

1. Recognize and believe in the powerful influence of television ministry. Know that being on television makes you known and makes your church visible. Being known and visible makes your church a good option whenever people are deciding to find a good church.

    There are times when people will attend your church as a direct response to your television programme.

    Be aware that your television programme will not necessarily cause more people to attend your church.

2. Decide to do television ministry only when the Lord has led you to do it. Always be led by the Spirit of God. Do not do things because everyone is doing them.

3. Spend the time to find out exactly what is involved in having a television ministry. There are many hidden costs in a television ministry.

4. Buy inexpensive equipment when you are a beginner in the television ministry. Do not listen to technical people who advise you to buy super expensive stuff that is not really necessary.

5. Train your own people to slowly learn the technical aspects of the television ministry. There is no rush. After you have trained ordinary people to do a television programme, your production cost will be almost zero. If you do not train your own people, you will have a very high production cost which will kill your television ministry.

6. Produce a quality television programme! Compare your programmes with other successful television ministries and try to match them. Emulation is the key to catching up and surging forward. Don't be ashamed to be a copy cat.

7. Always keep the name of your ministry on the screen. Show people how to reach you and make it easy for them to do so. Many people watch TV programmes for twenty minutes and do not know who is speaking or which ministry is being presented.

8. Develop an excellent website that will complement your television ministry. If you cannot be on television, you can have a website that shows your programmes. You may have more success on the website than on television. The internet will soon take over from what we know as television today.

9. Invite people to attend church, at the end of your programmes. Many people will come because you specifically asked them to. Use your time on television wisely. Tell people to come and see you in your church.

10. Have telephones and internet facilities available to respond to calls and requests that come from your television programme. Set up a system to respond promptly and eagerly to the people who call in. If you tell them to call in and they cannot reach you they will soon lose faith in your TV programme.

Steps to an Effective Bus Ministry

1. Be aware that the bus ministry could be the missing key from your church growth strategies

2. Know that buses help POOR PEOPLE to come to your church. Be aware of the blessings that come to people who help the poor. A church that considers the poor will receive many blessings.

3. Know that many of the largest churches in the world run effective bus ministries where they transport people from all over the city to their churches. Doing a bus ministry is simply following the example of many other mega churches in the world today.

4. Deploy buses to strategic points where you do outreaches. Let the people who have been saved and won to the Lord through your outreaches have an easy way of coming to the church.

5. Give free buses when you recognize that the people cannot pay for the service. Seek support for your bus ministry from the wealthier members of your church. In so doing the rich will be helping the poor.

6. Charge enough to cover your cost when they can pay for it so that the bus ministry does not ruin the finances of the church.

Section 18

CHURCH GROWTH TESTS

Chapter 41

Twenty Diverse Tests and Temptations of a Pastor Who Seeks Church Growth

Nothing is going to come to you easily. You must consider your life to be one long series of tests, trials and temptations. There is a purpose for each test that God takes you through. Because spiritual tests do not take place in a classroom they are not easily recognized. Many things that happen in our lives are actually tests! Your desire to have a mega church will lead you to a road that has many painful testing experiences.

Many things in a pastor's life look like coincidences but they are not. Many people you meet and interact with look like they just happened to come by. Indeed, they did not just come by; they were sent by the Lord. Some people you meet today are the newly arriving tests, trials and temptations of your life. You will be expected to pass the tests of relating with them. So what are the tests that a pastor of a mega church should expect to go through? What trials will a pastor desiring church growth experience?

Twenty Tests

1. **As you build a mega church, you will be tested so that you can be promoted. Without these tests you cannot be promoted.**

   In school, you cannot move to the next level unless you pass your tests. The scripture says that you become perfect and complete after you have successfully gone through trials, testings and temptations. O mega church pastor, don't you want to be perfect and complete? Don't you want to be fully qualified for all the increase that is coming to you?

Consider it all joy, my brethren, when you encounter various trials, knowing that the testing of your faith produces endurance. And let endurance have its perfect result, that you may be perfect and complete, lacking in nothing.

James 1:2-4, NASB.

2. **As you build your church, you will suffer persecution because you want to do something so godly as to build a big church.** Expect persecution from your friends, relatives, colleagues and bystanders. Don't complain because you are being persecuted. It's part of the package. Expect to be persecuted because of your mega church.

Yea, and all that will live godly in Christ Jesus shall suffer persecution.

2 Timothy 3:12

3. **In your quest for church growth, you will go through tests that are designed to humble you.** You need to be very humble to be a pastor of thousands of people. You must not think too highly of yourself. Expect troubles, persecutions, difficulties that will bring you to your knees.

Expect situations that you cannot do anything about to break you down, and bring you to your knees. O mega church pastor, these things are intended to help you remember that you are but a man.

And thou shalt remember all the way which the LORD thy God led thee these forty years in the wilderness, TO HUMBLE THEE, and to prove thee, to know what was in thine heart, whether thou wouldest keep his commandments, or no.

Deuteronomy 8:2

4. **In your quest for church growth, you will go through tests that will reveal what is in your heart.** No one knows what is really in your heart. You don't even know. But there are circumstances that can bring out what is in your heart.

God will allow those tests to reveal what is in your heart. You may say, "I love the Lord" but you really love a man. When the man is gone you will find out whether you really love the Lord.

And thou shalt remember all the way which the LORD thy God led thee these forty years in the wilderness, to humble thee, and to prove thee, TO KNOW WHAT WAS IN THINE HEART, whether thou wouldest keep his commandments, or no.

Deuteronomy 8:2

5. **In your quest for church growth, you will go through tests that will show whether you are really obedient.** "I love the Lord and I will obey Him" is the song of the average minister of the gospel. But there are certain things that will really reveal whether you are obedient to the Lord. It is easy to say, "I will go anywhere, I will do anything". Then the command will come, "Now go to the uttermost corner of that poor country!" Suddenly, all the obedience is thrown out of the window and you realize how unwilling and disobedient you really are. I have people who call me "Daddy" and answer every sentence with "Yes, please". They present themselves as the most humble and obedient servants. But one instruction can reveal how truly detestable and disobedient they really are.

    People profess, confess and claim things, but their deeds reveal that they are actually disobedient, detestable and worthless to you. "They profess to know God, but by their *deeds* they deny *Him*, being detestable and disobedient, and worthless for any good deed" (Titus 1:16, NASB). These are strong words but they are true.

6. **In your quest for church growth, you will go through tests to show whether you really love the Lord.** Do you really love the Lord? I love Jesus! I love the Lord with all my heart! I will do anything for Him. One day, something will come to your life and that thing will reveal what you love. Do you love the Lord, do you love money or do you

love the fame of ministry? It will all be revealed through the tests that are coming your way.

Thou shalt not hearken unto the words of that prophet, or that dreamer of dreams: for the LORD your God proveth you, TO KNOW WHETHER YE LOVE THE LORD YOUR GOD WITH ALL YOUR HEART AND WITH ALL YOUR SOUL.

Deuteronomy 13:3

7. **As you grow into a mega church pastor, you will go through tests that are like fiery trials.** Fire makes you lose everything. When you go through a trial that makes you feel that you are losing everything, don't be surprised. Don't think it is strange.

People have lost their wives, their children, their money and their self-respect through the fiery trials they experienced. Some people have lost as many as three wives in the fire. Some people lost as many as five children. You have to believe that these fiery trials are necessary for your promotion to a mega church pastor.

Beloved, think it not strange concerning the fiery trial which is to try you, as though some strange thing happened unto you:

1 Peter 4:12

8. **As you become a mega church pastor you will be tested by *bad winds*, bad storms and floods.** One day, the pastor of a large church said to me, "*A bad wind* is blowing on our friend."

He continued, "We must pray for him because if *that bad wind* turns in our direction, it will not be good for us!"

You see, as you build a mega church and work for God, you may think that only good winds will blow in your direction. The fact that you are doing the right things and building your house on a rock does not mean that a *bad wind* will not blow on you.

230

Amazingly, the *bad wind* that blows on the person who is doing all the wrong things is the same *bad wind* that will blow on the good person's house.

Therefore whosoever heareth these sayings of mine, and doeth them, I will liken him unto a wise man, which built his house upon a rock: And the RAIN descended, and the FLOODS came, and the WINDS blew, and beat upon that house; and it fell not: for it was founded upon a rock. And every one that heareth these sayings of mine, and doeth them not, shall be likened unto a foolish man, which built his house upon the sand: And the RAIN descended, and the FLOODS came, and the WINDS blew, and beat upon that house; and it fell: and great was the fall of it.

Matthew 7:24-27

9. **As you grow into a mega church pastor you will be tested with grief and sorrow.** Sadness, mourning and grief are tests that will meet every man desiring to be a mega church pastor. These are things that a mega church pastor must experience. By the time you have had a few heart-rending times of grief you will be wiser and more humble. You will become an eternity-oriented pastor because you *lay to heart* the times of mourning and grief. Without all these experiences your mind will gallop towards delusions that only end in more deception.

    It is better to go to the house of mourning, than to go to the house of feasting: for that is the end of all men; and the living will lay it to his heart."

Ecclesiastes 7:2

10. **A mega church pastor will be tested for his ability to withstand pressure.** A pastor of a big church is under a lot of pressure: pressure from the congregation, pressure from financial problems, pressure from his wife, pressure from his children, pressure from his associates, pressure from the dropping attendance, pressure from the projects, pressure from the employees, pressure from the press and pressure from the general public.

For we would not, brethren, have you ignorant of our trouble which came to us in Asia, that WE WERE PRESSED OUT OF MEASURE, above strength, insomuch that we despaired even of life:

2 Corinthians 1:8

11. **A mega church pastor will suffer temptations.** O mega church pastor you will not be exempted from temptations because of your lofty ambitions. You will be tempted in every way on your journey to achieving church growth. You will be tempted with finances to enrich yourself and to misuse money. You will be tempted with lustful things and strange women. You will be tempted with divorce. You will be tempted with disloyalty. You will be tempted with pride. You will be tempted with discouragement. You will be tempted to give up. You will be tempted with unforgiveness and bitterness. You will be tempted to misuse your power. Do not be deceived. The higher you go in the ministry, the more you should expect to be tested and tormented.

For we do not have a high priest who cannot sympathize with our weaknesses, but One who has been tempted in all things as we are, yet without sin."

Hebrews 4:15, (NASB)

12. **On your road to church growth, you will meet with wicked and unreasonable men.** O mega church pastor, get ready to meet unreasonable men and women who will oppose you and make things difficult for you. I have met men with an intractable dislike for us. There are people who have opposed the development of our cathedrals and church buildings. These unreasonable men are temptations and testing's on the way to your victory.

And that we may be delivered from unreasonable and wicked men: for all men have not faith.

2 Thessalonians 3:2

13. **A mega church pastor will be tested by people who desert him.** When people desert you, you will have to depend on the Lord. Along the journey of ministry, there will be many

who will abandon you. Don't cry too much when people leave you. I can tell you about quite a number of people who have deserted me especially as I went deeper into full time ministry.

It is not because you are a bad person that people abandon you. It is because of your calling and the tests that go with it.

For Demas, having loved this present world, has deserted me and gone to Thessalonica...

> 2 Timothy 4:10 (NASB)

14. **In your quest for church growth you will be tested by people who do not support you.** What a painful thing it is to have people withholding their support when you need it most.

At my first defense NO ONE SUPPORTED ME, but all deserted me; may it not be counted against them."

> 2 Timothy 4:16 (NASB)

15. **In your quest for church growth, you will be tempted with the personal weaknesses of your life.** Every pastor has personal weaknesses. Some have temperamental weaknesses which lead to moodiness, depression, and poor communication.

Other ministers suffer from disorganization, mismanagement of money and poor personal judgment. All these personal weaknesses show up as time goes on and present great temptations to the aspiring mega church pastor.

You will also be tempted with distressing situations. Many ministers have distressing marriages. The usual problems of marriage are heightened by the pressures of ministry and the pressures of pinnacle leadership.

Therefore I am well content with weaknesses, with insults, with DISTRESSES, with persecutions, with difficulties, for Christ's sake; for when I am weak, then I am strong.

> 2 Corinthians 12:10 (NASB)

16. **To become a mega church pastor, you must pass the test of handling disloyal people.**

How you handle disloyalty will determine how big your church can become. Disloyal people can scatter what you are building and make nonsense of your church growth efforts.

You will be tested on whether you can be drawn into confusion by strife-causing leaders.

Your understanding of loyalty and disloyalty will be revealed by your ability to improve or worsen complicated situations in the church.

You will be tested on your ability to silence the voice of the devil amongst your leaders. You will be tested on your ability to handle your accusers. You will be tested on your ability to dismiss people who bring division. You will be tested on your willingness to mark and avoid dangerous people.

Now I beseech you, brethren, mark them which cause divisions and offences contrary to the doctrine which ye have learned; and avoid them.

Romans 16:17

17. **In your quest to become a mega church pastor, you will struggle with your personal needs and the church's needs.** You will have needs that must be met and these needs and desires can become a test and a snare to you.

But in all things approving ourselves as the ministers of God, in much patience, in afflictions, in necessities, in distresses,

2 Corinthians 6:4

18. **In your quest to become a mega church pastor you will be tested with your ability to fast and pray as well as your ability to watch and pray.** Fasting is the painful activity of not eating so that you can pray. Watching is the painful activity of staying awake so that you can pray.

In weariness and painfulness, in WATCHINGS often, in hunger and thirst, in FASTINGS often, in cold and nakedness.

2 Corinthians 11:27

19. **In your quest for church growth you will be tested with your willingness to expose yourself to danger.** Many people have ended their journey to a great ministry because of dangers they did not want to expose themselves to. "Is it dangerous to go there?" they ask. In so doing, many people cut off themselves from the fields God expects them to work in.

It is the poor who are often open to the preaching of the gospel. These poor people who will come to your church, often live in dangerous and deprived areas. If you are not prepared to go to these poor and dangerous areas, there is very little you can do for God.

I have been on frequent journeys, in dangers from rivers, dangers from robbers, dangers from my countrymen, dangers from the Gentiles, dangers in the city, dangers in the wilderness, dangers on the sea, dangers among false brethren

2 Corinthians 11:26 (NASB)

20. **In your quest for church growth you will be tested for your susceptibility to delusions and deceptions.** As your church gets bigger and you have more money, you will be tested by the deceitfulness of riches. You will be tempted to despise small ministries and pastors of smaller churches. If you pass all these tests you will truly be ready to handle a mega church.

And for this cause God shall send them strong delusion, that they should believe a lie:

2 Thessalonians 2:11